Maritime Te

Risk and Liability

Michael D. Greenberg, Peter Chalk, Henry H. Willis,
Ivan Khilko, David S. Ortiz

AND CENTER FOR TERRORISM RISK MANAGEMENT POLICY

The research described in this report was conducted by the RAND Center for Terrorism Risk Management Policy.

Library of Congress Cataloging-in-Publication Data

Greenberg, Michael D., 1969–
    Maritime terrorism : risk and liability / Michael Greenberg, Peter Chalk,
Henry H. Willis, [et al.].
      p. cm.
    Includes bibliographical references.
    ISBN-13: 978-0-8330-4030-5 (pbk. : alk. paper)
    1. Merchant marine—Security measures. 2 Shipping—Security measures.
3. Passenger ships. 4. Container ships. 5. Terrorism—Prevention. 6. Pirates.
7. Hijacking of ships—Prevention. I. Chalk, Peter. II. Willis, Henry H. III. Title.

VK203.G74 2006
363.325'9387—dc22

                                              2006031873

The RAND Corporation is a nonprofit research organization providing objective analysis and effective solutions that address the challenges facing the public and private sectors around the world. RAND's publications do not necessarily reflect the opinions of its research clients and sponsors.

RAND® is a registered trademark.

Cover photo: Getty Images

Published 2006 by the RAND Corporation
1776 Main Street, P.O. Box 2138, Santa Monica, CA 90407-2138
1200 South Hayes Street, Arlington, VA 22202-5050
4570 Fifth Avenue, Suite 600, Pittsburgh, PA 15213-2665
RAND URL: http://www.rand.org/
To order RAND documents or to obtain additional information, contact
Distribution Services: Telephone: (310) 451-7002;
Fax: (310) 451-6915; Email: order@rand.org

The RAND Center for Terrorism Risk Management Policy (CTRMP)

CTRMP provides research that is needed to inform public and private decisionmakers on economic security in the face of the threat of terrorism. Terrorism risk insurance studies provide the backbone of data and analysis to inform appropriate choices for the government's role in supporting the terrorism insurance market. The research on the economics of various liability decisions informs the policy decisions of the U.S. Congress and the opinions of state and federal judges. Studies of compensation help Congress to ensure that appropriate compensation is made to the victims of terrorist attacks. Research on security helps to protect critical infrastructure and to improve collective security in rational and cost-effective ways.

CTRMP is housed at the RAND Corporation, an international nonprofit research organization with a reputation for rigorous and objective analysis and the world's leading provider of research on terrorism.

The center combines three organizations:

- RAND Institute for Civil Justice, which brings a 25-year history of empirical research on liability and compensation.
- RAND Infrastructure, Safety, and Environment, which conducts research on homeland security and public safety.
- Risk Management Solutions, the world's leading provider of models and services for catastrophe risk management.

For additional information about the Center for Terrorism Risk Management Policy, contact:

Robert Reville

RAND Corporation

1776 Main Street

P.O. Box 2138

Santa Monica, CA 90407

Robert_Reville@rand.org

310-393-0411, x6786

Michael Wermuth

RAND Corporation

1200 South Hayes Street

Arlington, VA 22202

Michael_Wermuth@rand.org

703-413-1100, x5414

A profile of the CTRMP, abstracts of its publications, and ordering information can be found at http://www.rand.org/multi/ctrmp/.

CTRMP Advisory Board

Kenneth R. Feinberg, Esq.
Managing Partner
The Feinberg Group, LLP

John Gorte
Executive Vice President
Dorinco/Dow Chemical

Ken Jenkins
Chief Underwriting Officer
American Reinsurance
RiskPartners

Hemant Shah
President and Chief Executive
Officer
Risk Management Solutions, Inc.

Cosette R. Simon
Senior Vice President
Swiss Re Life and Health America
Inc.

Steven A. Wechsler
President and Chief Executive
Officer
NAREIT

Preface

Intelligence analysts, law enforcement officials, and policymakers have become increasingly concerned about the possibility of future maritime terrorist attacks. The maritime environment possesses some unique characteristics that, in principle, could make it attractive to terrorist operations, including the extraterritoriality of the high seas and poor or inconsistent security measures that apply in coastal areas and facilities in many parts of the world. Maritime attacks have the potential to inflict significant harms on persons and property and, in at least some instances, could be highly disruptive to U.S. commerce.

This book focuses on the study of terrorism risk and liability issues in connection with two general types of maritime terrorism scenarios: attacks that target passenger vessels and attacks that target (or leverage) containerized shipping. With regard to analyzing risk, this book explores underlying threats, vulnerabilities, and potential consequences, and then combines this information to construct a picture of the relative risks posed by different terrorism scenarios. With regard to analyzing liability, this book outlines key concepts, legal authorities, and ambiguities that would apply in determining civil liability for acts of maritime terrorism, focusing particularly on third-party (commercial) defendants. By combining the investigation of risk and liability into a single study, this book offers insights both into the nature of maritime terrorism risk, as well as the ways in which government might respond to that risk through the instrumentality of the civil justice system. This book would be of interest to anyone who is concerned with understanding and managing maritime terrorist risks.

This version corrects errors in the book first posted on the RAND Web site in October 2006 and available through January 1, 2007. Errata associated with that version appear on the Web site. The corrections affect Figures 6.2, 6.3, 6.4, and 7.2 and Tables A.5 and A.6.

As a result of these corrections, the revised version of the book identifies an additional scenario as being high risk; USS *Cole*–style attacks involving ramming an improvised explosive device into a passenger ferry. This additional high-risk scenario is also reflected in the appropriate places in the text.

This research was funded by CTRMP, a partnership between RAND and Risk Management Solutions, Inc. CTRMP is funded by voluntary contributions from several organizations that represent property owners and other insurance purchasers, reinsurers, and insurers. An advisory board that included representatives of the donor organizations was invited to comment on the book, but RAND alone determined the scope, analytical methods, conclusions, and recommendations.

This research was conducted under the auspices of RAND Infrastructure, Safety, and Environment (ISE), a division of the RAND Corporation. The mission of RAND Infrastructure, Safety, and Environment is to improve the development, operation, use, and protection of society's essential physical assets and natural resources and to enhance the related social assets of safety and security of individuals in transit and in their workplaces and communities.

Questions or comments about this monograph should be sent to the project leader, Michael Greenberg (Michael_Greenberg@rand.org). Information about CTRMP is available online (http://www.rand.org/multi/ctrmp/). Inquiries about CTRMP projects should be sent to the co-directors:

Robert Reville
RAND Corporation
1776 Main Street
P.O. Box 2138
Santa Monica, CA 90407
Robert_Reville@rand.org
310-393-0411, x6786

Michael Wermuth
RAND Corporation
1200 South Hayes Street
Arlington, VA 22202
Michael_Wermuth@rand.org
703-413-1100, x5414

Contents

Figures

Tables

Summary

Policymakers have become increasingly concerned in recent years about the possibility of future maritime terrorist attacks. Although the historical occurrence of such attacks has been limited, concerns have nevertheless been galvanized by recognition that maritime vessels and facilities may (in some respects) be particularly vulnerable to terrorism. In addition, some plausible maritime attacks could have very significant consequences, in the form of mass casualties, severe property damage, and attendant disruption of commerce. Understanding the nature of maritime terrorism risk requires an investigation of threats, vulnerabilities, and consequences associated with potential attacks, as grounded both by relevant historical data and by intelligence on the capabilities and intentions of known terrorist groups. Assessment of the risks associated with maritime terrorism can help policymakers and private firms to calibrate and prioritize security measures, prevention efforts, and mitigation plans.

The risks associated with maritime terrorism also provide the context for understanding government institutions that will respond to future attacks, and particularly so with regard to the U.S. civil justice system. In principle, civil liability operates to redistribute the harms associated with legally redressable claims, so that related costs are borne by the parties responsible for having caused them. In connection with maritime terrorism, civil liability creates the prospect that independent commercial defendants will be held responsible for damages caused by terrorist attacks. Liability is thus a key aspect of the government's institutional response to terrorism, because (1) it creates strong incentives for private-sector prevention and mitigation efforts, (2) it serves as a foundation for insurance to spread related risks, and (3) it defines the scope and likelihood of compensatory transfer payments from firms to victims.

This book explores the nature of maritime terrorism risks associated with a limited set of attack scenarios involving passenger and container shipping. The book also examines U.S. civil liability rules as they may apply in the context of these types of attacks.

Risk Assessment: Threat, Vulnerability, and Consequences

Our analytic strategy for addressing the risks associated with attacks on passenger and container shipping began from a broad assessment of related threats and vulnerabilities, based on a combination of historical data regarding previous attacks, and on a series of interviews with counterterrorism experts. We then investigated the likely consequences that would follow from different modes of attack, drawing on historical data and publicly available analyses, and by framing those consequences in terms of human effects (e.g., casualties), economic effects (e.g., property damage and business disruption), and intangible effects (e.g., political and governmental responses). Finally, we combined the information on threat, vulnerability, and consequences to generate estimates of relative risk, in connection with attack scenarios involving ferries, cruise ships, and container shipping. Our qualitative method for generating these risk estimates involved the use of defined ordinal scales to assess terrorists' intents and capabilities, target vulnerabilities, and attack consequences. This method is described in detail in the appendix.

With regard to attacks on ferries, our findings suggest that on-board bombings present the greatest combination of threat and vulnerability among the specific types of assaults that we considered. In terms of consequences, all of the attack modes targeting ferries involve roughly comparable estimates of potential economic harm, but on-board bombings are projected to be somewhat less invidious in inflicting human casualties than two other modes of assault (parasitic bombing, and ramming attacks involving improvised explosive devices [IEDs]). With regard to attacks on cruise ships, we considered a broader range of likely attacks, and found that on-board bombings, followed by standoff artillery assaults and food or water contamination scenarios, present the greatest combination of threat and vulnerability. Once again, all of the attack modes targeting cruise ships involve roughly comparable estimates of potential economic harm, but parasitic bombings, ramming attacks with IEDs, and biological attacks (i.e., those involving contamination of a ship's food or water supply) are projected as presenting somewhat greater potential for harm in the form of human casualties.

With regard to attacks on containerized shipping, we note that cargo vessels themselves are attractive primarily as a means to transport weapons or to sabotage commercial operations more broadly, rather than as a direct target for terrorist assaults per se. This being said, most scenarios we considered had comparable combinations of threat and vulnerability. The economic consequences associated with any maritime assault that shuts down operations at a major U.S. port could be severe. A dirty-bomb attack perpetrated using an illicit cargo container presents the greatest combination of likelihood and expected economic harm. In terms of human consequences (i.e., casualties), most container shipping scenarios present a low likelihood of inflicting such harms, and the prospect of relatively modest human consequences even where that likelihood is realized. Perhaps most notably, container shipping scenarios involving nuclear detonations are less likely than the other scenarios we considered, but could entail far greater potential consequences in both human and economic terms.

Civil Liability and Maritime Terrorism

Our analysis of civil liability connected with maritime terrorist attacks draws primarily on a review of legal authorities, related materials, and scholarly commentaries addressing the topic. Our aim in conducting this review was to accomplish three things: first, to identify major issues that arise in analyzing maritime terrorism liability problems; second, to describe some of the key legal rules (and ambiguities) that will likely apply in future cases; and third, to analyze some of the implications for potential victims, commercial defendants, and insurers. As a threshold matter, civil liability is important both because it operates to transfer some of the costs associated with attacks from victims to other parties and because it creates private-sector incentives for prevention and mitigation efforts. By corollary, civil liability contributes directly to the magnitude of financial risks that firms confront in participating in maritime commerce. Civil liability also comprises the primary, well-established government mechanism for compensating victims.[1]

Analyzing civil liability in the context of future acts of maritime terrorism is complex, and it depends significantly on the facts involved in particular attacks. Nevertheless, several of the major steps involved in any such analysis are clear. The first question that arises involves the location of an attack and the circumstances leading up to it. Most attacks occurring in U.S. waters or territory and on the high seas are likely to be subject to U.S. jurisdiction and, in many instances, may be subject to federal admiralty rules that will determine liability standards. The second analytic question that arises simply involves identifying who is likely to be hurt in a hypothetical attack, and how: The nature of the harm defines the pool of potential plaintiffs and the types of the claims that they may bring. Subsequent steps in analyzing terrorism liability involve looking in detail at U.S. admiralty rules, at the substantive legal standards that they establish, and at the limits of their scope of application.

The central tort issue that will likely arise in connection with future maritime terrorist attacks involves the extent to which commercial defendants can be held liable for the independent criminal acts of terrorists. Traditional legal doctrines have tended to define the scope of negligence liability in terms of preventing "foreseeable" risks, with the result of substantially limiting liability for criminal acts committed by third parties (these mostly being viewed as unforeseeable). But in the

---

[1] Notably however, this mechanism was partially bypassed in the wake of September 11, through special federal legislation that created a compensation fund for victims (49 USCS 40101).

wake of September 11, the standard of foreseeability as applied to terrorist attacks is far from clear, and conceivably could be expansive. As a result, current tort liability risks associated with maritime terrorism are fundamentally ill-defined, but potentially quite large.

Key Observations and Recommendations

Based on the findings of our investigations into maritime terrorism risk and liability, we offer the following set of conclusions and recommendations for policymakers:

- The greatest risks involving container shipping stem from scenarios involving radiological or nuclear detonation, or the extended disruption of operations at a port. *For radiological or nuclear detonation, effective risk management approaches must include securing nuclear materials at their points of origin.* Checking cargo containers moving through the container shipping system is impractical and imperfect because of the large number of containers and the inherent errors (both false positives and false negatives) of inspection technologies. The risks from extended disruption of ports are largely economic. *These risks are most effectively reduced through planning to facilitate the restart of ports and container shipping systems in the wake of a terrorist attack or natural disaster.*
- The greatest risks involving cruise ships and passenger ferries stem from cruise ship scenarios involving on-board bombs or food or water supply contamination and passenger ferry scenarios involving on-board bombs and USS *Cole*–style improvised explosive device attacks. Because it is essential that people be allowed to move freely on these types of vessels, it would be difficult to eliminate the risks completely. *The most effective approach for minimizing the risks, however, involves reducing the vulnerabilities of ferries and cruise ships, by auditing the soundness of vessel and facility security practices, by improving security measures at ports for passengers and luggage, and by implementing rigorous procedures for documenting crew and staff.*
- Many perceptions of maritime terrorism risks do not align with the reality of threats and vulnerabilities. First, there is little evi-

dence that terrorists and piracy syndicates are collaborating. The economic motivations for piracy (which depend for fulfillment on the stability of maritime trade) may be in direct conflict with the motivations of terrorists (i.e., in achieving maximum disruptive effects in connection with attacks). Second, some plausible forms of maritime terrorism (e.g., sinking a cargo ship in order to block a strategic lane of commerce) actually present relatively low risk, in large part because the targeting of such attacks is inconsistent with the primary motivation for most terrorist groups (i.e., achieving maximum public attention through inflicted loss of life). Third, any effort to sink a freight or cruise ship would need to overcome engineering designs intended to prevent catastrophic failure of a ship's hull. Experts believe that improvised explosive devices would have limited capability to cause such failure. *Maritime terrorism policy should not be motivated by these perceived threats.*

- Civil liability is a key aspect of the government's institutional response to maritime terrorism. Liability operates to redistribute some of the harms associated with an attack from victims to other parties who bear legal responsibility for those harms. Because terrorist perpetrators are often a poor prospect for recovery in civil suits seeking compensation for victims, third-party firms and property owners are likely to be targeted in postattack tort litigation. *As a result, firms engaged in maritime commerce need to recognize that they operate at risk and should investigate the extent of their own tort liability.*

- Civil liability standards in maritime terrorist attacks against the United States will likely draw on specialized rules in admiralty, particularly with regard to attacks on ferries and cruise ships. Related rules include liability standards for personal injury and death, regulatory requirements pertaining to vessel security, and statutory limits on liability for vessel owners. *Admiralty jurisdiction over these sorts of claims may preempt competing legal rules that would otherwise apply on land and may limit the compensation that can be sought by victims in some circumstances. Policymakers should review these rules to confirm their appropriateness in application to future terrorist attacks.*

- Maritime attacks that leverage cargo containers could target port facilities or inland locations, and subsequent supply chain disruptions could implicate a host of contractual and tort disputes. *To the extent not already standard practice, parties to commercial contracts should specifically consider and address terrorism risks in connection with those contracts.*

- A key issue in tort liability for future maritime attacks will involve the extent to which third-party defendants (i.e., firms and property owners) can be held liable for the independent actions of terrorists. The same fundamental issue could arise in connection with a host of statutory and common law rules. The traditional criterion of foreseeability in negligence provides little guidance, in the wake of the September 11 attacks, regarding the scope of related responsibilities for potential defendants. *Policymakers should carefully review the scope and rationale of third-party liability for terrorist attacks, both in regard to providing reasonable compensation to victims and in setting appropriate incentives for prevention and mitigation efforts by private firms. More broadly, policymakers should consider the pros and cons of liability as a method for dealing with terrorism risks and injuries.*

Acknowledgments

The authors thank the many officials and security analysts in the United Kingdom and Singapore who cooperated with the RAND research team to make data and insights available. We are also grateful to Robert Reville, Michael Wermuth, Brian Jackson, and K. Jack Riley of RAND, and to several members of the CTRMP board, for their input and suggestions regarding our work. We would like to acknowledge Maria Falvo for her dedication and patience and in helping us to prepare the manuscript.

Several reviewers provided thoughtful comments that strengthened this book.

Abbreviations

ABOT	Al Basrah oil terminal
APCSS	Asia Pacific Center for Security Studies
ASG	Abu Sayyaf Group
ATSSSA	Air Transportation Safety and System Stabilization Act
CBR	chemical, biological, or radiological
CBRN	chemical, biological, radiological, or nuclear
COGSA	Carriage of Goods by Sea Act
CSCAP	Council for Security Cooperation in the Asia Pacific
CSI	Containerized Shipping Initiative
C-TPAT	Customs-Trade Partnership Against Terrorism
CTRMP	Center for Terrorism Risk Management Policy
DFLP	Democratic Front for the Liberation of Palestine
DOHSA	Death on the High Seas Act
FISA	Foreign Intelligence Surveillance Act
FSP	facility security plan
GAM	Gerakan Aceh Merdeka

GSP	gross state product
ICSC	International Council of Shopping Centers
IED	improvised explosive device
IMB	International Maritime Bureau
IMO	International Maritime Organization
ISPS	International Ship and Port Facility Security
JI	Jemaah Islamiyah
JWC	Joint War Council
KAAOT	Khawr Al Amaya oil terminal
LHWCA	Longshore and Harbor Workers' Compensation Act
LNG	liquefied natural gas
LTTE	Liberation Tigers of Tamil Eelam
LVOLA	Limitation of Vessel Owner's Liability Act
MTSA	Maritime Transportation Security Act
P&I	property and indemnity
PA	Palestinian Authority
PFLP-GC	Popular Front for the Liberation of Palestine–General Command
PIJ	Palestinian Islamic Jihad
PIRA	Provisional Irish Republican Army
PLF	Palestine Liberation Front
PSI	Proliferation Security Initiative
QEII	Queen Elizabeth II
RFID	radio frequency identification

RPG	rocket-propelled grenade
RSRM	Rajah Soliaman Revolutionary Movement
SAM	surface-to-air missile
SCTC	Senior Counter-Terrorism Course
SLOC	sea-lane of communication
SOLAS	Safety of Life at Sea
SUA	Convention for Suppression of Unlawful Acts Against the Safety of Maritime Navigation
TIR	Trans International Routier
TRIA	Terrorism Risk Insurance Act of 2002
UCC	Uniform Commercial Code
UNCLOS	United Nations Convention on the Law of the Sea
VSP	vessel security plan

CHAPTER ONE

Introduction

With the collapse of the Soviet Union and the European Communist bloc in the late 1980s, it was widely assumed that the international system was on the threshold of unprecedented peace and stability. Politicians, academics, and diplomats alike began to forecast the establishment of a "new world order" that would be managed by liberal democratic institutions. It was assumed that as this new structure emerged and took root, destabilizing threats to national and international security would decline commensurately.

However, the initial euphoria evoked by the end of the Cold War has been replaced by growing recognition that global stability has not been achieved and has, in fact, been decisively undermined by transnational security challenges. These new threats cannot readily be defeated by the traditional defenses that states have erected to protect their territories and their citizenry. Stated another way, the current geopolitical landscape lacks the relative stability of the linear Cold War division between East and West. Few of today's dangers have the character of overt military aggression stemming from a clearly defined sovereign source. By contrast, security, conflict, and threat definition have become far more opaque and diffuse in nature, often taking the form of amorphous challenges, "gray area phenomena," and acts of politically motivated violence by groups unaffiliated with sovereign governments, operating outside the mainstream of the international community.

The maritime realm is particularly conducive to these types of threat contingencies, given its vast and largely unregulated nature. Covering more than 130 million square miles of the earth's surface, most of the planet's maritime environment takes the form of high seas that lie beyond the strict jurisdiction of any one state—meaning that they are, by definition, anarchic. A complex lattice of territorial waters, estuaries, and riverine systems, which in many cases are poorly monitored, fringe and link these oceans. The basic characteristics of the maritime environment have increasingly galvanized concern on the part of academics, intelligence analysts, law enforcement officials, and politicians about the possible exploitation of the maritime realm to facilitate terrorist logistical and operational designs. Indeed, commentators in several countries now appear to believe that the next major terrorist strike against Western interests is as likely to emanate from a nonterritorial theater, as from a land-based one. The potential leverage of the maritime domain for violent acts of political extremism presents a host of challenges for policymakers in the United States and abroad. This book aims to address some of these challenges by providing a better understanding of (1) the nature of maritime terrorist threats and corresponding vulnerabilities; (2) the potential consequences that might follow from an attack; (3) the interplay between threat, vulnerability, and consequences in determining maritime risk; and (4) the manner in which U.S. civil liability institutions might respond in the aftermath of a maritime terrorist attack.

Analyzing Maritime Terrorism: Threat, Vulnerability, Consequences, and Liability

The threshold step in any complete analysis of maritime terrorism involves a detailed examination of threat. The marine environment lends itself to a broad range of plausible attack scenarios. By examining how these possible contingencies might manifest, assessing their operational implications, and exploring their relationship to historical attacks and the characteristics of known terrorist groups, we can generate an empirically based foundation for characterizing the risks confronted by sovereign states across the globe. An analysis of this sort has particular relevance and salience for the United States, in that it will help to anchor policy decisions about how best to secure and manage the nautical domain (proactively as well as reactively), and how to apportion risks and costs associated with potential attacks in the future.

While discussion of terrorist threats is very important, a full account of maritime risks also requires consideration of the vulnerability of nonterritorial platforms and systems to attack or exploitation. More specifically, the design and operation of maritime vessels and facilities, together with related security procedures, are integral to any assessment of the likelihood of success for terrorist attempts to strike at, or leverage, different types of targets. Just as important, infrastructure vulnerability is critical to informing the development (and prioritization) of future mitigation and deterrence measures, in a manner that is both rational and cost-effective.

The scope of ramifications for a maritime terrorist event targeting American interests is wide. At the most immediate level, consequences of an attack could include casualties and loss of life, property damage, and economic disruption. Even bounding what those consequences might look like across a range of attack scenarios presents a significant challenge, given limitations in available empirical data and analogous historical events. Nevertheless, an attempt to determine the consequential "footprint" of maritime strikes is very important, largely because attack implications are an essential part of the risks that government and business interests are already confronting and seeking to mitigate and manage.

When taken together, the assessment of threats, vulnerabilities, and consequences of maritime terrorism plays a key role in defining the nature of the terrorism risks that the U.S. faces, and the relative importance of different attack scenarios for purposes of structuring protective measures and remediation mechanisms.[1]

But analysis of the full risks associated with hypothetical maritime terrorist attacks goes even beyond threat, vulnerability, and consequences. Potential strikes occur against a backdrop of existing government institutions and business interests that have some responsibility for preventing those assaults. Once an attack actually takes place, the

---

[1] For previous discussion of a conceptual "threat, vulnerability, consequences" framework for estimating terrorism risks, see Willis et al. (2005).

same institutions and interests become focal to efforts to compensate the damages and to rebuild. The U.S. civil justice system is the basic institution that defines the scope of legally redressable claims in the United States, providing a mechanism for victims to seek compensation from parties responsible for their injuries. The civil justice system also operates to create incentives in the private sector for taking appropriate precautions and for obtaining insurance to spread risks. Thus, a third dimension in analyzing potential maritime terrorist attacks involves examining the likely application of civil liability rules to those assaults. This kind of liability analysis determines the extent to which many of the costs of an attack are likely to be transferred from immediate victims to other persons and business interests. For companies engaged in maritime commerce, the liability dimension of terrorism is important because it defines both private-sector accountability for anticipating attacks and financial responsibility for harms in their wake.[2] For government policymakers, the liability dimension raises an additional set of concerns, particularly in relation to whether legal rules are clear as applied to terrorist attacks and whether the rules are likely to result in appropriate compensation to victims and incentives for the private sector.

A complicating feature of liability in connection with maritime terrorist attacks involves unique legal and jurisdictional issues that arise concerning events that occur on navigable waterways. In particular, to the extent that some plausible terrorism scenarios involve attacks on the high seas, those scenarios are fundamentally extraterritorial in nature, creating ambiguity as to what jurisdiction or substantive laws might apply to them. Moreover, for attacks occurring on American territorial waters, it is likely that U.S. admiralty law will apply in determining liability. This legal regime involves its own set of technical requirements, precedents, and standards, independent of other federal and state laws that might be used to ascertain civil liability for other sorts of terrorist strikes. For these reasons, the analysis of liability problems connected

---

[2]   As we discuss in Chapter Four, ambiguous liability standards underscore the reality that specific terrorist attacks are difficult to foresee in detail and, in consequence, that firms may be held accountable for events that they cannot realistically anticipate.

with maritime terrorism is unique, although some of the lessons to be learned might well have broader application with regard to other terrorist contingencies.

Businesses engaged in maritime commerce confront the problem of taking appropriate security measures to prevent and mitigate attacks, and to fulfill legal duties of care to potential victims. In practice, that means that those companies must assess and respond to terrorist threats and consequences, in light of the accountability standards imposed by civil liability rules. In the absence of liability, commercial interests would have no financial responsibility for terrorism-related harms to third parties, and by implication, would bear only limited risks and operating costs associated with possible maritime attacks. Unlimited liability, on the other hand, would mean that businesses would bear complete responsibility for all possible terrorism-related harms to third parties, which would necessarily entail far higher risks and, presumably, much greater operating costs. In short, understanding the private sector implications of maritime terrorism requires a consideration of threat, consequences, *and* liability. Only then can the implications for maritime commerce be fully appreciated and evaluated in light of broader social interests pertaining to the protection of trade, the prevention of attacks, and the provision of compensation to victims.

At the outset, we acknowledge that, apart from civil liability in tort, many other aspects of policy and legal doctrine will also contribute to the government's response to future terrorist attacks and, consequently, to risks and incentives for the private sector. For example, bankruptcy and state corporation laws exemplify other legal regimes that have the power to shift the costs of an attack between persons who are injured by it (i.e., victims) and those who might otherwise be held responsible for it (i.e., firms and their owners). We do not here attempt to analyze fully all of the policy and legal issues that are likely to influence terrorism compensation or that may affect the financial risks that maritime firms will confront in connection with future terrorist attacks. Instead, we have limited our focus to civil liability issues. We believe that these issues are particularly important, for several reasons. First, civil liability establishes fundamental standards for whether victims will have any rights to recover in tort and, consequently, whether firms will be forced to bear corresponding financial risk. These basic legal standards are complicated and ambiguous in their own right, and can be viewed as imposing their own set of risks and uncertainties on firms and victims in connection with terrorism. Second, civil liability also establishes the legal foundation for other sorts of risk-transfer and risk-sharing mechanisms. This is most notably true of the private insurance market, where tort liability determines whether (1) firms will be compelled to insure against terrorist harms to third-party victims or (2) potential victims will need to self-insure against terrorism risks. Finally, the application of tort liability in connection with terrorist attacks raises basic questions about the soundness of the civil justice system as a mechanism for dealing with terrorism risk. Where attacks have the potential to result in mass litigation, perverse incentives for private firms, and uncertain or delayed compensation for victims, the application of civil liability standards to such attacks demands close scrutiny.

Focus on the Problem: Exploring Attacks Against Passenger and Container Shipping

The focus of this book is to study terrorism risk and liability issues in connection with two general types of maritime terrorism scenarios: attacks that target passenger vessels and attacks that target (or that leverage) container shipping. We note at the outset that there are other possible forms of maritime terrorist events that we do not address here, such as attacks targeting liquefied natural gas (LNG) tankers. Our current focus is limited because we believe that attacks on passenger and container shipping represent two of the most important and realistic categories of potential maritime terrorist events. Although the findings we present here serve to illuminate the nature and implications of attacks on passenger and container shipping, they also highlight an analytical framework that could be applied to the study of other sorts of terrorist events.

In the text that follows, note that much of the examination of threat draws on international data concerning historical maritime terrorist attacks and related groups. By contrast, the analysis of liability issues focuses specifically on U.S. laws and, by implication, on hypo-thetical terrorist events that would either affect or occur within U.S. territory. Because the analysis of threat necessarily relies significantly on historical data, and because virtually all maritime terrorism activity to date has occurred outside the United States, any study of seaborne threats will necessarily focus in large part on international events and foreign terrorist groups. The findings presented here are nevertheless relevant to U.S. security, because threats against maritime targets in U.S. territory would require either (1) an expanded scope of activity by foreign nationals or (2) the emergence of new domestic terrorist groups with maritime capabilities not currently known. With regard to explor-ing civil liability issues, we deliberately limit our investigation here to U.S. law, because questions regarding the application of foreign liabil-ity rules to overseas attacks are extremely complicated and would likely vary depending on the legal framework of a specific nation targeted in an attack. Thus, our analysis on liability issues pertains most directly to attacks occurring in the United States (or on U.S. targets on the high seas). That said, the methodological approach adopted here also serves to illustrate some of the basic legal concepts and liability problems that will likely arise in the context of attacks occurring elsewhere in the world.

In the remainder of this book, we address risk and liability in connection with maritime terrorist attacks on or involving passenger and containerized shipping. Chapter Two provides a broad overview of the nature of maritime terrorist threats and associated vulnerabil-ities, based on historical and interview data. Chapter Three offers a taxonomy for analyzing the consequences of maritime terrorist events involving passenger and containerized shipping. Chapter Four assesses the manner in which U.S. civil liability rules and jurisdiction would apply in the wake of a maritime terrorist event and ties some of the key issues in liability to the facts of a particular attack. Chapters Five, Six, and Seven use the components of the previous analyses to assess the respective terrorist risk to container vessels, cruise liners, and ferries. Finally, Chapter Eight offers a discussion of some of the main implica-tions gleaned from the analyses of threat, consequences, and liability. Chapter Eight concludes with a list of key observations and recommendations to policymakers, intended to facilitate understanding and management—partly through the mechanisms of private-sector civil liability—of the risks posed by terrorist attacks on passenger and container shipping.

CHAPTER TWO

The Contemporary Threat of Maritime Terrorism

Intelligence analysts, law enforcement officials, and policymakers have become increasingly concerned in recent years about the possibility of terrorist groups carrying out attacks in the maritime realm. The Council for Security Cooperation in the Asia Pacific (CSCAP) Working Group has offered an expansive definition for the types of events that comprise maritime terrorism:

> . . . the undertaking of terrorist acts and activities (1) within the maritime environment, (2) using or against vessels or fixed platforms at sea or in port, or against any one of their passengers or personnel, (3) against coastal facilities or settlements, including tourist resorts, port areas and port towns or cities. (Quentin, 2003)

Yet despite the breadth of this definition, the world's oceans have not historically been a major locus of terrorist activity. Indeed, according to the RAND Terrorism Database, seaborne strikes have constituted only 2 percent of all international incidents over the last 30 years. What explains the apparent contradiction between current concerns regarding maritime terrorism and existing evidence of terrorist activity?

To answer this question, this chapter evaluates the potential threats of maritime terrorism. We begin by discussing the factors underscoring the current concern with this particular manifestation of militant extremism and the reasons that might motivate terrorists to undertake operations in a marine environment. We then briefly examine the main terrorist organizations that have actually operated at sea, summarizing some of the key strikes that have been linked to these various groups.

Factors Underscoring the Contemporary Perceived Threat of Maritime Terrorism: Vulnerability, Capability, and Intent

It should perhaps not be surprising that until now terrorists have neglected to exploit maritime targets. In the past, maritime terrorism did not correspond well to terrorists' available opportunities, capabilities, or intentions. Many terrorist organizations have neither been located near to coastal regions nor possessed the necessary means to extend their physical reach beyond purely local theaters. Even for those groups that did have a geographic opportunity, there are several problems associated with carrying out waterborne strikes that have, at least historically, worked to offset some of the tactical advantages of the maritime environment.[1]

Operating at sea requires terrorists to have mariner skills, access to appropriate assault and transport vehicles, the ability to mount and sustain operations from a non–land-based environment, and familiarity with certain specialist capabilities (for example, surface and underwater demolition techniques).[2] Limited resources have traditionally precluded such options being available to most groups.

The inherently conservative nature of terrorists in terms of their chosen attack modalities compounds the constraints imposed by limited opportunities and lack of technical skills. Precisely because groups are constrained by ceilings in operational finance and skill sets, most have deliberately chosen to follow the course of least resistance— adhering to tried and tested methods that are known to work, which

---

[1]   Again, the advantages to terrorists of maritime settings include the fundamentally anarchic nature of "over the horizon" oceans, together with frequently lax security monitoring over coastal waters, riparian systems, and related facilities and infrastructure.

[2]   Anonymous Institute of Defense and Strategic Studies representative (2005). See also Wilkinson (1986) and Jenkins et al. (1986).

offer a reasonably high chance of success, and whose consequences can be relatively easily predicted. Stated more directly, in a world of finite human and material assets, the costs and unpredictability associated with expanding to the maritime realm have typically trumped any potential benefits to terrorists that might have been garnered from initiating such a change in operational direction.

A further consideration has to do with the nature of maritime targets themselves. Since many maritime targets are largely out of sight (something that is particularly true of oceangoing commercial vessels), they are relatively speaking also out of mind. Attacking a ship is, thus, less likely to elicit the same publicity—in either scope or immediacy—as striking land-based venues, which, because they are fixed and typically located near some urban conglomeration, are far more media-accessible (although as is argued below, this may be less true with respect to contingencies involving heavily laden cruise liners and ferries) (Wilkinson, 1986, p. 34; Jenkins et al., 1986, p. 65). This consideration is important, since terrorism, at root, is a tactic that can only be effective if it is able *visibly* to demonstrate its salience and relevance through the so-called propaganda of the deed.[3]

Despite these considerations, the perceived threat of maritime terrorism has risen markedly over the last several years and is now taking on a singular importance in terms of national and international counterterrorism planning.[4] This is particularly true of the United States, which has been at the forefront of attempts to strengthen the global regime of maritime security in the post–September 11 era. The reasons for this heightened level of apprehension are complex and multifaceted, but generally pertain to concerns that can be grouped in terms of vulnerability, capability, and intent.

---

[3] For a discussion on this aspect of the terrorist phenomenon see Chalk (1996, Chapter One). Rather like the philosopher's conundrum regarding the unobserved tree that falls in a forest (i.e., does it make a sound?), one might raise a similar question regarding the effect of an unwitnessed and unpublicized terrorist attack: Does it really accomplish a political purpose?

[4] Anonymous former British defense official and Department of Homeland Security Liaison attache (2005). See also Frittelli (2004, pp. 1–3); Wrightson (2005, pp. 1, 7).

Vulnerability of Maritime Targets

The international community appears to have become progressively more cognizant of the general vulnerability of global shipping as a result of the largely unpoliced nature of the high seas, the fact that many littoral governments lack the resources—and in certain cases, the willingness—to enact serious programs of coastal surveillance, and the sheer esoteric character that typifies much of the oceanic environment. As Rupert Herbert-Burns of Lloyd's of London observes:

> The combination of the enormous scope, variety and "room for maneuver" offered by the physical and geographical realities of the [earth's] maritime environment . . . presents a sobering and uncomfortable reality. . . . [W]hat compounds this reality further is that the commercial milieu that simultaneously affords . . . the ability to deploy, finance operations, tactical concealment, logistical fluidity and wealth of targets of opportunity—the commercial maritime industry—is itself numerically vast, complex, deliberately opaque and in a perpetual state of flux. (Herbert-Burns, 2005, p. 158)

Exacerbating international concern is the increased dependence of seaborne commercial traffic (which itself has risen markedly over the last five to ten years)[5] on passing through narrow and congested maritime choke points, where, owing to forced restrictions on speed and maneuverability, vessels remain highly vulnerable to offensive interception.[6] Such misgivings have been especially palpable in light of moves by a growing number of shipping companies to replace full staffing

---

[5]   More than 6 million containers enter U.S. ports every year, which accounts for nearly half of the world's present inventory (12–15 million containers are estimated to be moving on the world's oceans at any given point in time). See Sinai (2004, p. 49).

[6]   Key choke points of concern include the straits of Malacca, Bab el Mandeb, Hormuz, Bosporus, Dardanelles, Dover, and Gibraltar, and the Suez, Panama, and Keele canals. All of these waterways require ships to reduce speed significantly to ensure safe passage (in the Bosporus Strait, for instance, at least six accidents occur every 1 million transit miles); are vital to global commercial, passenger, and military shipping; and constitute viable locations from which to launch maritime attacks using contiguous land-based platforms. Anonymous former British defense official (2005). See also Köknar (2005).

complements with "skeleton" crews—sometimes numbering no more than half a dozen personnel—as a cost-cutting device. Although this practice has helped to lower overhead operating costs, it has also made gaining control of ships that much easier.

Certain vessels have also been highlighted as remaining particularly vulnerable to deliberate sabotage. As is discussed at greater length in the next chapter, passenger ferries are often singled out in this regard, largely because they tend to be characterized by extremely lax predeparture security screening of passengers, sail according to preset and widely available schedules, and, at least in the case of ships that transport vehicles, necessarily lack stabilizing bulkheads on their lower decks (anonymous UK customs and excise officials, Raytheon and Glenn Defense Marine analysts, and Control Risks Group officials, 2005).

Capability of Terrorist Groups

The inherent openness and opaqueness of the maritime environment has been viewed as particularly worrisome during a time when terrorist capabilities to act on a nonterritorial "footing" may be increasing. Two broad issues have been raised. First, various commentators have argued that the growth of offshore industries combined with the general popularity of maritime sports is serving to expand greatly the potential ease by which groups can gain basic skills and equipment for seaborne attacks.[7] The southern Philippines is often taken as a salient case in point. Here, suspected members of Jemaah Islamiyah (JI) are known to have enrolled in scuba courses run by commercial or resort diving companies, which members of the security forces widely believe have been undertaken for the specific purpose of facilitating underwater attacks against gas and oil pipelines off the coast of Mindanao.[8]

---

[7] See, for instance, Jenkins et al. (1986, p. 67).

[8] Anonymous defense antiterrorism and intelligence officials and Anti-Terrorism Task Force officials (2005). What appears to have particularly attracted the attention of Philippine and American security personnel is that the alleged JI members actively sought training in deep-sea water diving but exhibited little or no interest in decompression techniques.

Second, there is a general fear that terrorists could overcome existing shortcomings in seaborne attack capabilities by contracting out to pirate syndicates. Most concern in this regard has focused on the possible employment of maritime crime groups to hijack and deliver major ocean-going vessels (such as oil tankers, container ships, and LNG carriers), which might then either be scuttled to block critical sea-lanes of communication (SLOCs) or detonated to cause a major explosion at a target port of opportunity. While the possible convergence between piracy and terrorism remains highly debatable—not least because these actors are motivated by differing and, in many ways, conflicting objectives[9]—it is a contingency that has been highlighted in several maritime threat assessments over the past five years and is clearly one that security, intelligence, and maritime officials are not prepared to dismiss out of hand (Frittelli, 2004, p. 8; Raymond, 2005, p. 197; Sinai, 2004, p. 51; "ASEAN," 2002; Ijaz, 2003). A case in point was the Lloyd's Joint War Council (JWC) 2005 designation of the Malacca Strait as an "Area of Enhanced [Terrorism] Risk."[10] This determination was based on a disputed threat-vulnerability study carried out by the UK-based Aegis group, which specifically considered anticipated future links between regional Islamist militants and maritime criminals in its analysis.[11]

---

[9]   The "business" of piracy, for instance, depends directly on a thriving and active global shipping industry while contemporary terrorists associated with the international jihadist network generally seek to disrupt maritime trade as part of their self-defined economic war against the West. The incompatability of these objectives was repeatedly expressed to the authors during interviews with Ministry of Foreign Affairs and Ministry of Home Affairs officials and Control Risks Group analysts (2005).

[10]   The designation of the Malacca Strait as an area of enhanced risk allows maritime insurance companies to levy a "war surcharge" on ships transiting the waterway up to 0.01 percent of the total value of their cargo; this is over and above the 0.05-percent baseline premium that is routinely imposed on seaborne freight. At the time of writing, no shipping association had actually been required to make the additional payment. Notably, while the Malacca Strait was included on the Lloyd's list of designated regions and countries, Syria, Iran, Sri Lanka, and Yemen were all taken off. The JWC reviews each designation quarterly (anonymous Lloyd's of London analysts, 2005).

[11]   Anonymous Lloyd's of London analysts (2005). It should be noted that both Singaporean and Western maritime security and intelligence officials dismissed the validity of the Aegis report, noting that the group has no recognized analytical presence in the region and that its

Intent of Terrorist Groups

For several reasons, government and intelligence personnel believe contemporary terrorist groups may be actively seeking to extend operational mandates to the maritime environment. On one level, there is an argument that extremists groups could see utility in instituting sea-based activities as a means for overcoming extant security measures on land, the comprehensiveness of which has dramatically escalated over the last several years. Certainly while heightened internally based immigration and customs arrangements and general target-hardening have emerged as staples of counterterrorism in many countries since September 11, 2001, the overall latitude of action on the world's oceans and coastal waters remains prevalent, offering extremists the opportunity to move, hide, and strike in a manner not possible in a terrestrial theater (Herbert-Burns, 2005, p. 157). In many ways, this process of threat displacement has arguably been further encouraged by international pressure on littoral states to invest in territorially bounded homeland security initiatives. In the case of governments that have consistently struggled to enact effective systems of coastal surveillance (for example, the Philippines, Indonesia, Turkey, Eritrea, and Kenya), such external demands have negatively impacted already limited resources for offshore surveillance (anonymous Raytheon and Glenn Defense Marine analysts and Control Risks Group personnel, 2005). Policy analysts contend that the resultant void would be of particular interest to terrorist groups, given their asymmetric relationship with state adversaries and, therefore, their need to opt for operational environments that are most conducive to their tactical designs (anonymous former defense intelligence official, 2005).

Maritime attacks may also hold an increasing degree of attractiveness in that they have emerged as an alternative means for potentially causing mass economic destabilization. Today roughly 80 percent of global freight moves by sea, much of which takes the form of cargo that is transshipped on the basis of a "just enough, just in time" inventory.

---

assessment was not in line with the empirical risk of attack (terrorist or pirate) in the Malacca Strait (especially when one compares the number of incidents that have occurred with the volume of traffic passing through the strait).

Disrupting the mechanics of this highly intensive and efficient trading system has the potential to trigger vast and cascading fiscal effects, particularly if the operations of a major commercial port were severely curtailed.[12] As Michael Richardson explains,

> The global economy is built on integrated supply chains that feed components and other materials to users just before they are required and just in the right amounts. That way, inventory costs are kept low. If the supply chains are disrupted, it will have repercussions around the world, profoundly affecting business confidence. (Richardson, 2004, p. 7)

Attacking petroleum tankers and offshore energy facilities has been similarly highlighted in terms of generating significant economic externalities.

The suicide attack against the M/V *Limburg* in October 2002 is frequently emphasized as representing a pertinent case in point. Although the incident resulted in only three deaths (two of which were the bombers'), it directly contributed to a short-term collapse of international shipping business in the Gulf of Aden and nearby waters, led to a $0.48/barrel hike in the price of Brent crude oil and, as a result of the tripling of war-risk premiums levied on ships calling at the Aden, caused the Yemeni economy to lose an estimated $3.8 million a month in port revenues.[13]

The disruptive economic dimension of maritime terrorism has been singled out as having specific pertinence to al Qaeda precisely because Osama bin Laden has emphasized that attacking key pillars of the Western commercial and trading system is integral to his self-defined war on the United States and its major allies. Certainly there have been repeated statements attributed to the Saudi renegade and his major cohorts post–September 11, which have explicitly denigrated America as a paper tiger on the verge of financial collapse, with many

---

[12] Anonymous Control Risks Group (UK) personnel (2005). See also Raymond (2005, p. 179).

[13] See Sheppard (2003, p. 55), Richardson (2004, p. 70), Herbert-Burns (2005, p. 165), and Chalk et al. (2005, p. 22, fn. 20–21).

further urging young Muslims to wage their jihad against Washington by focusing on targets that are liable to have a disruptive economic effect, including shipping (Eedle, 2002; Campbell and Gunaratna, 2003, pp. 73–74; Jehl and Johnston, 2004). This stance was perhaps best exemplified in an al Qaeda communiqué that was issued following the bombing of the M/V *Limburg*:

> By exploding the oil tanker in Yemen, the holy warriors hit the umbilical cord and lifeline of the crusader community, reminding the enemy of the heavy cost of blood and the gravity of losses they will pay as a price for their continued aggression on our community and looting of our wealth.[14]

Besides economic fallout, maritime security experts point to the potential of sea-based terrorism as a further means for inflicting "mass coercive punishment" or triggering a major environmental disaster.

In terms of inflicting coercive punishment, cruise ships and passenger ferries are commonly accepted as representing viable venues for executing large-scale civilian-centric strikes. These types of vessels move and cater to large numbers of people and, at least in the case of luxury liners, they often represent high-prestige, symbolic targets (anonymous former defense intelligence official, 2005). Moreover, thanks to international media and satellite communications, it is now far more probable that these types of attacks will elicit the necessary exposure and publicity that terrorists crave. As one British naval expert put it, "Should a cruise ship be bombed—even in the middle of vast oceans—one can expect that news teams would be on the scene covering the story, if not within minutes, certainly within hours."[15] Even if this were not the case, the advent of modern video technology has provided terrorists with a ready means to record and transmit their messages of death and destruction, as has been so vividly demonstrated with the televised images of beheadings of Westerners in Iraq since 2003.

---

[14] Alleged bin Laden statement cited in Herbert-Burns (2005, p. 165). See also Whitaker (2002).

[15] Comment made during the Senior Counter-Terrorism Course (SCTC), Asia Pacific Center for Security Studies (APCSS), Honolulu, September 1, 2005.

With regard to creating potential environmental disasters, government officials and environmental groups contend there is good reason to speculate that a decisive terrorist strike could result in extensive ecological damage and, quite possibly, instability. These commentators argue that because heavy crude oil will not disperse or easily emulsify when treated with detergents, a major spill from a stricken petroleum tanker is liable to devastate the marine environment in the immediate vicinity of the release and, if left to drift, could conceivably degrade elongated stretches of fertile coastline (Richardson, 2004, p. 42). For some developing states in Africa and Asia that rely heavily on fish for both indigenous consumption and overseas export earnings, such effects have the potential to feed into wider socioeconomic unrest and could possibly act as a trigger for political instability.[16] Although deliberately causing environmental harm has yet to emerge as a mainstream terrorist tactic, it is certainly one that analysts have postulated as a potential motivator for future acts of extremism, particularly as militants seek to extend the focus of their aggression toward venues that have historically not factored significantly in national or international security planning.[17]

Security analysts note with alarm that these various rationales are already becoming manifest in the sense that not only are international terrorists exhibiting greater tactical sophistication and innovation than in the past—perhaps best exemplified by the September 11 strikes[18]—a growing number also appear to be broadening their militant agendas to include specific experimentation with seaborne modalities. Indeed as Table 2.1 highlights, no fewer than five major maritime terrorist events have taken place since 2000. The main fear is that these inci-

---

[16] Asia is particularly prone to effects such as these, not least because popular perceptions of governing legitimacy often rest on the ability of the central administration to provide socioeconomic prosperity.

[17] See, for instance, Penders and Thomas (2002).

[18] The sophistication and innovation of September 11 was reflected in several respects: the coordination of multiple aircraft hijackings; long-term planning and surveillance on the part of the perpetrators—much of which was undertaken in hostile, enemy territory; the institution of an effective logistics support infrastructure that literally spanned the globe; and the ability to mount simultaneous, mass casualty attacks using conventional weapons.

dents may be indicative of a future trend in militant Islamist extremism that increasingly views the maritime realm as both a viable and conducive theater of activity.[19]

Table 2.1 catalogs some of the higher-profile and publicized incidents connected to these groups.

Contemporary Maritime-Capable Terrorist Groups

Several groups have already recognized the inherent advantages of operating at sea and moved conspicuously to integrate waterborne modalities into their overall logistical and attack mandates. The following have been among the better known of these organizations:

- PIRA, which has conspicuously exploited commercial shipping to avail the resupply of weaponry and other war-related materiel[20]
- Chechen rebels, who have carried out sporadic attacks against passenger ferries in the vicinity of the Bosporus Strait
- Al-Gama'a al-Islamiyya, which carried out strikes against passenger ships during the early to mid-1990s
- Palestinian organizations, including Hamas, Palestinian Islamic Jihad (PIJ), PA, the Popular Front for the Liberation of Palestine–General Command (PFLP-GC), the Democratic Front for the Liberation of Palestine (DFLP), and PLF. The latter group carried out the infamous hijacking of the *Achille Lauro* in 1985, which remains, arguably, one of the most spectacular seaborne assaults to date.

---

[19] Anonymous Control Risks Group (UK) personnel and Maritime Intelligence Group analyst (2005). See Sinai (2004, pp. 50–51).

[20] Many of these weapons were procured from Libya and transported to Ireland in container vessels fraudulently registered under flags of convenience. In the course of one year during the late 1980s, PIRA took delivery of nearly 120 tonnes of arms and explosives through this conduit, including AK47 assault rifles, Webley pistols, rocket-propelled grenade (RPG) launchers, surface-to-air missiles (SAMs), hand grenades, and a wide assortment of ammunition, detonators, fuses, and SEMTEX-H explosives. See Chalk (1996, p. 42) and "Arming the IRA" (1990).

Table 2.1
High-Profile Maritime Terrorism Incidents, 1961–2004

Incident	Group	Deaths	Remarks
Hijacking of *Santa Maria* (1961)	Portuguese and Spanish rebels	N/A	The *Santa Maria*, a 21,000-ton cruise ship owned by Companhia Colonial of Lisbon, was hijacked by a group of 70 men led by Captain Henriques Galvao (a Portuguese political exile) to bring global attention to the Estado Novo in Portugal and related fascist regime in Spain. The vessel was on a holiday cruise in the southern Caribbean and its more than 600 passengers were held for 11 days before Galvao formally surrendered to the Brazilian navy. The incident constitutes the first modern-day hijack at sea. [a]
Use of a Cypriot-registered coaster, *Claudia*, to transport weapons to Ireland (1973)	Provisional Irish Republican Army (PIRA)	N/A	*Claudia* was intercepted by the Irish Navy while attempting to land a consignment of weapons intended for PIRA. On board were five tons of munitions that included 250 Soviet-made assault rifles, pistols, mines, grenades, and explosives. The vessel was owned by Gunther Leinhauser, a West German arms trafficker, which said that PIRA had given him a "shopping list" of required materiel and that the "order" had been filled by Libya (Wilkinson, 1986, p. 39).
Hijacking of *Achille Lauro* (1985)	Palestine Liberation Front (PLF)	1	Cruise ship hijacked in an attempt to coerce the release of 50 Palestinians being held in Israel. The perpetrators were eventually detained in Sicily. Person killed was Leon Kling-hoffer, a German, wheelchair-bound tourist, who was captured by the world's media as he was pushed overboard. [b]
Targeting of cruise ships on the Nile River (1992–1994)	Al-Gama'a al-Islamiyya	N/A	The group targeted at least four cruise ships during these two years as part of its general effort to undermine the Egyptian tourist sector (a key contributor to the country's economy) (Sinai, 2004, p. 50; Sitilides, 1998).
Hijacking of a Turkish passenger ferry in the Black Sea (1996)	Chechen rebels	N/A	Nine rebel gunmen held 255 passengers hostage for four days during which they threatened to blow up the captured ferry in order to bring international attention to the Chechen cause; the abductors eventually sailed the vessel back to Istanbul where they surrendered. [c]

Table 2.1—Continued

Incident	Group	Deaths	Remarks
Suicide bombing of the USS Cole (2000)	Al Qaeda	19	The bombing took place while the Cole was refueling at the Yemeni port of Aden. The assault involved 600 pounds of C4 explosive that was packed into the hull of a suicide attack skiff. Those killed were 17 U.S. sailors, 2 terrorists. In addition to the 17 sailors who were killed, another 39 were injured.[d]
Suicide bombing of the M/V Limburg (2002)[e]	Al Qaeda	3	The attack involved a small, fiberglass boat packed with 100–200 kg of TNT rammed into the tanker as it was preparing to take on a pilot-assisted approach to the Ash Shihr Terminal off the coast of Yemen. The Limburg was lifting 297,000 barrels of crude at the time of the strike, an estimated 50,000 of which spilled into the waters surrounding the stricken vessel. Those killed were 1 crewman and 2 terrorists.
Use of Karine A to transport weaponsAuthority (PA) for anti-Israeli strikes (2002)	Palestinian Authority (PA)	N/A	Karine A, a 4,000-ton freighter, was seized in the Red Sea on January 3, 2002. The vessel was carrying a wide assortment of Russian and Iranian arms, including Katyusha rockets (with a 20-kilometer range), antitank missiles (LAW and Sagger), long-range mortar bombs, mines, sniper rifles, ammunition, and more than two tons of high explosives. The US$100 million weapon consignment was linked directly to Yasir Arafat and was allegedly to be used for attacks against Jewish targets in Israel and the Occupied Territories ("IDF Seizes PA Weapons Ship," 2002).
Hijacking of the M/V Penrider, a fully laden shipping fuel oil tanker from Singapore to Penang in northern Malaysia (2003)	Gerakan Aceh Merdeka (GAM)	N/A	This is one of the few instances where GAM has directly claimed responsibility for a maritime attack. The group took three hostages (the master, chief engineer, and second engineer), who were eventually released after a $52,000 ransom was paid.[f]

Table 2.1—Continued

Incident	Group	Deaths	Remarks
Use of the *Abu Hassan*, an Egyptian-registered fishing trawler, to transport weapons and training manuals to assist militant strikes in Israel	Lebanese Hezbollah	N/A	The Egyptian owner of the trawler was recruited by Hezbollah and trained specifically to carry out maritime support missions. The vessel, which Israeli naval commandos intercepted 35 nautical miles off Rosh Hanikra near Haifa, was being used to ferry a complex weapon and logistics consignment, consisting of fuses for 122mm Qassam rockets, electronic time-delay fuses, a training video for carrying out suicide strikes, and two sets of CD-ROMs containing detailed bomb-making information (Herbert-Burns, 2005, p. 166).
Attacks against the Khawr Al Amaya oil terminal (KAAOT) and Al Basrah oil terminal (ABOT), Iraq (2004)	Jamaat al-Tawhid	3	The attacks were claimed by al Zarqawi as a follow-up to the 2000 *Cole* and 2002 *Limburg* strikes (using the same small-craft, suicide modality) and appeared to be part of an overall strategy of destabilization in Iraq (the terminals were shut down for two days, costing nearly US$40 million in lost revenues) (Warouw, 2005, p. 12; Köknar, 2005).
Bombing of the Philippine *SuperFerry 14* (2004)	Abu Sayyaf Group (ASG), combined with elements from Jemaah Islamiyah (JI) and the Rajah Soliaman Revolutionary Movement (RSRM)[9]	116	Attack involved 20 sticks of dynamite that were planted in a hollowed-out television set. The bomb set off a fire that quickly spread throughout the ship due to the lack of an effective internal sprinkler system. Of the 116 fatalities, 63 have been identified (at the time of writing) and 53 remain unaccounted for. The incident has been listed as the most destructive act of terrorism in maritime history and the fourth most serious international incident since September 11, 2001 (anonymous Anti-Terrorism Task Force officials, 2005).

Table 2.1—Continued

Incident	Group	Deaths	Reamrks
Suicide attack against the Port of Ashdod, Israel (2004)	Hamas, al-Aqsa Martyr's Brigade	10	The attack took place at Ashdod, one of Israel's busiest seaports, and involved two Palestinian suicide bombers from Hamas and the al-Aqsa Martyr's Brigade. The perpetrators had apparently been smuggled to the terminal inside a commercial container four hours before the operation. Some speculation remains that al Qaeda assisted with logistics of the strike (Köknar, 2005).

[a] Jenkins et al. (1986, p. 69); "Santa Maria Hijacking" (undated). The hijacking was also known as "Operation Dulcinea" by the hijackers.

[b] The PLF's original intention was to seize the *Achille Lauro* and then ram it into the Israeli oil terminal at Ashad. However, the attack team was discovered before this operation could be put into effect, forcing a change in plan (anonymous security and terrorism analyst, 2005).

[c] Sinai (2004, p. 50); Sitilides (1998); Köknar (2005); "Hostage Taking Action by Pro-Chechen Rebels Impairs Turkey's Image" (2001). Allegedly the gunmen had also considered blowing up one of the two suspension bridges that cross the Bosporus to close the Strait to traffic.

[d] For more on this incident, see Perl and O'Rourke (2001).

[e] The M/V *Limburg* has since been renamed and now operates under the designation M/V *Maritime Jewel* (anonymous International Maritime Bureau personnel and Maritime Intelligence Group analyst, 2005).

[f] Herbert-Burns (2005, pp. 167–168). See also McGeown (2003) and International Maritime Organization (2003).

Table 2.1—Continued

9 JI is an Indonesia-based jihadist group that has been linked to al Qaeda and allegedly seeks the creation of a pan-regional Islamic caliphate in Southeast Asia. It has been held responsible for several high-profile attacks in the region, including the 2002 Bali bombings (which collectively killed 198 people and remains the single most deadly international terrorist attack since September 11, 2001), suicide strikes on the U.S.-owned Marriott Hotel and Australian Embassy in Jakarta between 2003 and 2004 (with a combined toll of 17 deaths and 248 injuries), and coordinated attacks against tourist hubs, again in Bali, in 2005 (32 killed, over 100 wounded). For two excellent overviews of the group's origins and terrorist activities, see ICG (2002, 2003). The RSRM is a highly fanatical fringe element of Balik Islam, a Philippines-based movement composed of Christian converts to Islam. The group has been linked to both JI and ASG and seeks to replace the existing administration in Manila with a Muslim theocracy to purge what it regards as the artificial influx of Catholic influences first introduced by the Spanish and then consolidated under the Americans (anonymous antiterrorism and intelligence officials, 2005). See also Villaviray (2003) and "Summary of Report" (2004).

- Lebanese Hezbollah, which is known to have received training in seaborne techniques from its principal sponsor, Iran, and has made efficient use of the maritime environment for covertly moving weapons, personnel, and materiel[21]
- ASG, which has been responsible for numerous seaborne strikes in the southern Philippines—including the 2004 sinking of *Super-Ferry 14*. Resulting in 116 fatalities, this incident remains the most deadly act of maritime terrorism to have been carried out in the modern era (although it appears as though the extent of the death toll was more "accidental" than deliberate—see Table 2.1).
- GAM, which, prior to its signing of a peace agreement with the Indonesian government in 2005, had been linked to a number of hijackings of tugs, fishing trawlers, and other small craft in the Strait of Malacca[22]
- the Liberation Tigers of Tamil Eelam (LTTE), which, in the guise of the group's so-called Sea Tigers, retains the most advanced maritime attack capability of any known substate terrorist insurgency (see the appendix for a detailed discussion of the unit's structure and operations)
- Jamaat al-Tawhid wa'l-Jihad (or Unity and Jihad Group), a Sunni organization led by Abu Musab al-Zarqawi until his death in June 2006 that has been at the forefront of attacks against U.S.-led coalition forces in Iraq
- al Qaeda, which was behind the bombing of the USS *Cole* in 2000 and the French-registered M/V *Limburg* two years later. Prior to his arrest in 2003, the movement's chief maritime plan-

---

[21] Anonymous Institute of Defense and Strategic Studies representative (2005). According to a former member of British defense intelligence, Hezbollah has also acquired a Soviet-era patrol boat that it uses for its own coastal "policing" purposes (anonymous former defense intelligence official, 2005).

[22] It should be noted that many commentators do not view these strikes as terroristic, as their prime motivation is economic. However he i that seized funds have been used specifically to support GAM's insurgency in Ace ge that the attacks represent something more than basic criminality and do, in fact, i lve a definite political dimension that Herbert-Burns has termed "logistical-support terrorism." See Herbert-Burns and Zucker (2004) and Raymond (2005, p. 197).

ner, Abdel Rahim al-Nashiri (colloquially known as Ameer al Bahr, or "Prince of the Sea"), was also believed to have been in the latter stages of finalizing plans to attack Western shipping interests in the Strait of Gibraltar.[23] More recently, in August 2005, a Syrian national linked to al Qaeda, Lu'ai Sakra, was linked to a plot to ram explosive-laden speedboats into cruise ships carrying Israeli tourists to Turkey (Ant, 2005; "World Briefing Middle East," 2005).

• Various allegations have additionally surfaced pertaining to the existence of an al Qaeda fleet of ocean-going vessels. According to Lloyd's List and a 2002 Norwegian intelligence report, for instance, prior to September 11, the organization owned at least 23 ships, most of which operated through front companies located in Liberia, Tonga Panama, Belize, and the Isle of Man (all notorious for tolerating registration bureaus that permit irresponsibly lax strictures regarding crewing conditions and documentation requirements) (Köknar, 2005; "What al-Qaida Could Do with 'Terror Navy,'" 2003). A similar U.S. report has put al Qaeda's inventory at 15 merchant carriers, which may or may not include other ships chartered but not specifically owned by the network.[24] There have also been periodic reports that bin Laden has used fishing trawlers procured from family businesses located in Madagascar and parts of Asia to transport weapons, ammunition, and explosives (Sinai, 2004, p. 58). Definitive evidence to back these various claims, however, has never materialized and as such they should necessarily be treated with an air of caution.

---

[23] Percival (2005, p. 9), Richardson (2004, p. 19), Köknar (2005), "Al-Qaeda Has Multi-Faceted Marine Strategy" (2003), Smith (2004). Nashiri had apparently developed a four-point plan for the attacks in the Mediterranean, which included ramming ships with small boats; detonating medium-sized vessels near other craft or at port; crashing aircraft into large carriers such as supertankers; and using suicide divers or underwater parasitic devices (for example, submersible limpet mines) to destroy surface platforms.

[24] See Sakhuja (2002); Raymond (2005, p. 193); Herbert-Burns (2005, pp. 171–172); Sinai (2004, p. 58); Grier and Bowers (2003); Mintz (2002); and "Al-Qaida Training Manual Shows Seaports Top Target" (2003). According to one former British defense official, al Qaeda owns only one or two ships outright, with most of its assets taking the form of charter vessels (anonymous former defense intelligence official, 2005).

Scenarios of Potential Maritime Terrorist Activity in the Future

Looking to predict how terrorists may actually seek to exploit the maritime realm for future operational purposes, intelligence analysts and security experts have highlighted several scenarios in their analytical forecasting. At least seven possibilities are routinely postulated:

- use of a commercial container ship to smuggle chemical, biological, or radiological (CBR) materials for an unconventional attack carried out on land or at a major commercial port such as Rotterdam, Singapore, Hong Kong, Dubai, New York, or Los Angeles
- use of a "trojan horse," such as a fishing trawler, resupply ship, tug, or similar innocuous-looking vessel, to transport weapons and other battle-related materiel
- hijacking of a vessel as a fund-raising exercise to support a campaign of political violence directed toward ethnic, ideological, religious, or separatist designs
- scuttling of a ship in a narrow SLOC in order to block or disrupt maritime traffic
- hijacking of an LNG carrier that is then detonated as a floating bomb or used as a collision weapon
- use of a small, high-speed boat to attack an oil tanker or offshore energy platform to affect international petroleum prices or cause major pollution
- directly targeting a cruise liner or passenger ferry to cause mass casualties by contaminating the ship's food supply, detonating an on-board or submersible improvised explosive device (IED) or, again, by ramming the vessel with a fast-approach, small, attack craft.[25]

A thorough discussion of all these contingencies is beyond the scope of this analysis. However, to give a flavor of extant vulnerabili-

[25] Anonymous former defense official and Control Risks Group (UK) personnel (2005). See also Campbell and Gunaratna (2003, pp. 70–89), Herbert-Burns (2005, pp. 163–169), Sinai (2004, pp. 63–64), and Percival (2005, pp. 10–13).

ties and potential opportunities that might be available to terrorists wishing to operate in the maritime realm in the near to medium term, Chapters Five, Six, and Seven of this book are devoted to assessing the risks posed in connection with three specific types of shipping targets: cruise liners, passenger ferries, and container vessels.

These types of shipping targets were selected in part because they receive a great deal of public attention and for two additional reasons. First, attacks against passenger vessels have already occurred and constitute the most frequent occurrence of terrorism in the maritime realm. Second, as years of drug trafficking bear witness, it is relatively easy to compromise the integrity of the oceanic container network for smuggling purposes. Thus, container shipping is vulnerable to terrorists' attempts to smuggle goods.

CHAPTER THREE

Consequences of Maritime Terrorism

Passenger and commercial shipping in the maritime domain are both large and highly profitable industries in the United States. Their size and importance alone make it worthwhile to estimate the potential consequences of terrorism to these industries.

Both the U.S. and global economies depend on commercial shipping. U.S. ports handle approximately 20 percent of worldwide maritime trade. The value of national and international products transported through the United States annually is approximately $9.1 trillion, with the international component of that being roughly $2 trillion (almost half of which is container-transported materials). Moreover, the international tonnage of trade transported through the United States is expected to double by 2020, tripling the volume currently transported through the East Coast ports and quadrupling that currently transported through the West Coast ports (Foschi, 2004, pp. 1–46).

Passenger ships, meanwhile, are used in the United States for both commuting and leisure travel. More than 66 million passengers travel by ferry each year in the United States, with the largest ferry systems operating in the Seattle/Tacoma, New York/New Jersey, New Orleans, Boston, and San Francisco Bay areas (American Public Transportation Association, 2006). More than 9 million passengers board cruise ships each year in North America, contributing approximately $14.7 billion to the U.S. economy (Business Research and Economic Advisors, 2005).

Given the foregoing, attacks involving U.S. passenger or container shipping clearly have the potential to affect large numbers of people and important sectors of the U.S. economy. The types of consequences that could be expected after an attack on passenger or container shipping can be broadly defined in terms of who is affected, how they are affected, and by how much they are affected. This chapter provides an ontology to address the first two of these issues. Since the magnitude of attack effects is scenario specific (i.e., dependent on the nature of a particular attack), the last issue is addressed separately through case studies of maritime risks in cruise-, ferry-, and container-related attacks, provided in Chapters Five, Six, and Seven of this book.

Parties Affected by Maritime Terrorism

The distribution of the consequences of maritime terrorist attacks may be just as relevant to public policy as their magnitude. Terrorist attacks can destroy property that is exclusive to individuals or private firms. Attacks can likewise affect the public sector, by destroying public property and by interfering with revenue sources that provide for public goods and services.

In drawing a similar distinction among the parties affected by terrorism, Jackson and Dixon (2005) distinguish how the scope and motivations of investment decisions differ between individuals, private-sector firms, and public-sector institutions. According to microeconomic theory, individuals act to maximize personal welfare to the extent their resources allow. Similarly, firms maximize the profit generated through the value of present and future revenues. This is in contrast to the assumed responsibility of the public sector to maximize welfare of society as a whole, occasionally through the redistribution of goods, services, and wealth.

Categorizing the consequences of terrorism in terms of its effects on individuals, private-sector firms, and public-sector institutions can help to frame issues of distribution. For example, the distribution of effects across these three sets of parties can influence perceived equity in the aftermath of an attack. The public may view a terrorist attack that predominantly contaminates houses of people living near an industrial facility but who are not employees of the facility very differently than it would a cyberattack that destroys only the infrastructure of a single private firm.

In some important respects, the consequences of a terrorist attack to individuals, private firms, and the public sector are unlikely to be independent. This is true in the obvious sense that the lives lost in a terrorist attack simultaneously involve catastrophic harm to the individuals involved and a loss of human capital to the businesses or agencies that employ them. On a more esoteric level, though, government policies can also have the effect of *redistributing* some of the consequences of an attack in a manner that may shift related burdens among individuals and private-sector firms. For example, under applicable workers' compensation laws, most businesses are required to insure their employees against injury while working. This insurance lessens the burden of accidental injury to victims, by shifting a portion of related costs to private firms, under administrative oversight by government. In a similar manner, civil liability is another mechanism for redistributing the burden of injuries among individuals, private firms, and government agencies.

Although the operation of these kinds of cost-shifting policy mechanisms might itself be construed broadly as a "consequence" in the wake of a terrorist attack, the mechanisms can also be understood independently as a complex set of rules and procedures for limiting, preventing, or remediating some of the effects of hypothetical attacks. In this book, we address the civil liability implications of potential maritime terrorist attacks separately and in detail in Chapter Four. For current purposes, it suffices to emphasize that the public-sector effects of terrorism may include both immediate harms to public institutions and assets in the wake of an attack, as well as secondary cost-shifting effects through the operation of public institutions like the civil justice system.

Connecting Consequences to Terrorist Events

Whether or not presumed consequences can be observed is affected by the proximity of the causal link between the terrorist event and presumed consequences. *Direct* consequences manifest themselves in the form of loss of human life, physical destruction of property caused by the physical and biological effects of a terrorist event, and response and recovery from the attack.

Many other *indirect* consequences subsequently result from these effects. Businesses may be unable to operate because of policing and infrastructure damage around them. Individuals and businesses depending on those directly affected by an attack may suffer disruptions as a result. Individual and firm decisionmaking may change because of psychological reactions to the consequences of an event. Broader consequences can continue to ripple outward as these disruptions propagate, and individual and firm decisionmaking is influenced by the occurrence of terrorism.

The indirect consequences of terrorism are difficult to estimate. Jackson and Dixon (2005) appropriately noted that the distinction between direct and indirect effects can be quite ambiguous. The magnitude of indirect effects depends on how broadly the scope of a terrorist event is defined. Considering only those entities physically affected and connecting effects in adjacent communities will result in different estimates than would result, for example, from also considering effects on businesses across the nation that suffer logistical disruptions.

As the causal chain of events stretches, it also becomes increasingly difficult to attribute behavior to a particular event.[1] There are two explanations for this. One is that manifestation of indirect consequences depends on choices that individuals and organizations make in response to an event. A company that sits and waits for its supplier to recover may lose significant business, but one that places a replacement order from an unaffected supplier may not suffer at all. How people and organizations do, in fact, respond when faced with par-

---

[1]   Note that the U.S. civil justice system has long grappled with the problem of bounding the limits of causal relationships in the context of compensating tort claims. Beyond the general observation that indirect causes are often subjective in interpretation and difficult to apprehend fully, the law has frequently taken the position that some categories of injury (e.g., harm to future income in the absence of loss of property or physical or psychological injury) will simply not be compensated in tort, by virtue of the fact that causal relationships involved may be too distant to justify it.

ticular terrorist events is not well understood, making it difficult to estimate these indirect consequences. A second explanation is that, as the causal proximity grows more distant, effects might fade into the noise of other events shaping economic activity. For example, supplier disruptions that might be expected to limit supply of a commodity and raise prices may be offset by an unrelated oversupply of the same commodity.

As an alternative to distinguishing between direct and indirect costs, Jackson and Dixon (2005) captured causal relationships between events and consequences by considering attack costs, security and preparedness costs, and costs resulting from behavioral change. Where relevant in the chapters that follow, we describe our estimates of the consequences of terrorist acts in terms of these three types of costs, again as experienced by individuals, private firms, and the public sector.

Types of Consequences of Maritime Terrorism

The consequences of maritime terrorism can manifest in many forms. Table 3.1 presents a summary of the types of consequences of maritime terrorism that might affect individuals, the private sector, and the public sector. Broadly, these consequences fall into one of three groups: *human*, *economic*, and *intangible* effects.

Human consequences refers to effects on lives caused by fatalities and injuries. *Economic consequences* are those effects easily quantified in financial terms. *Intangible effects* capture those effects that are difficult to measure in human lives or financial metrics either because they are measured in metrics that are not easily translated into lives or financial metrics or because the cause-and-effect linkage is not understood well enough to allow precise estimation and attribution of effects.

Human Consequences of Terrorism

Individuals carry the ultimate burden of the consequences of terrorism. It is people who are injured or killed and who suffer debilitating psychological consequences following terrorist attacks. Moreover, the indirect consequences of fatalities and injuries can flow into both

Table 3.1
The Scope of Consequences of a Maritime Terrorist Attack

Affected Party	Human Consequences	Economic Consequences	Intangible Consequences
Individuals	Fatalities Injuries	Loss of salary Loss of property Loss of investments Loss of public services	Psychological consequences leading to changes in saving, earning, and consumption preferences
Private sector		Destruction of property Ships Facilities Transportation infrastructure Products and raw materials Loss of data Life and injury compensation Short-term disruption of business cycle Immediate lag in delivery Loss of customers Loss of revenue business interruption Increased transport costs Internal diseconomies of scale Long-term transportation inefficiency Augmented security measures Increased insurance rates	Loss of human capital in the private sector Changes in consumption and investment preferences Reduced tolerance of risky investments Loss of future revenue streams Decreased foreign confidence Decreased foreign investment Increased cost of foreign trade because of insecurity Shifts in stock market Decrease in tourism and resulting losses in revenue
Public sector		Loss of revenue for government Destruction of public infrastructure Financial costs of response and recovery Increased government spending on counterterrorism	Political consequences Loss of human capital in the public sector

the public and private sectors, particularly in terms of economic costs. Again, the costs associated with fatalities and injuries may be transferred, at least in part, through compensatory mechanisms like insurance and civil tort claims, with some of the burdens associated with human injuries borne by the private sector.

In addition, fatalities affect both the public and private sectors in terms of loss of human capital. To the public sector, this most frequently results in a temporary loss of capability (a diseconomy of scale) until organizations can be reorganized. If a large proportion of people with a particular specialty skill (such as nuclear power plant design) or serving a specific function (such as elected government) were affected by a terrorist attack, the results could be severely disruptive and could potentially take years from which to recover. In the private sector, loss of human capital that would not affect the nation's production capabilities can be devastating to individual firms. For example, in the World Trade Center attacks on September 11, 2001, 658 employees of the investment firm of Cantor Fitzgerald died, leading to the collapse of Cantor Fitzgerald's core interdealer business in the United States (Cantor Fitzgerald, undated).

Economic and Intangible Consequences of Property Damage

Terrorist attacks can destroy both physical and intellectual property. Attacks that damage facilities, ships, vehicles, airplanes, infrastructure, or products and raw materials reduce the assets of private firms. In cases in which power is disrupted or computer networks are targeted, loss of data may also reduce firm assets that enable future revenues.

Damage to infrastructure, facilities, and information systems may propagate into both short- and long-term economic disruptions. Firms may immediately experience delivery delays, loss of revenue from interrupted business, and increased transportation costs. Reduction of demand or supply could eliminate the benefits of economies of scale until facilities and infrastructure can be replaced. As the magnitude and duration of disruptions to infrastructure, facilities, and information systems increase, the consequences can be more permanent. Firms may experience long-term transportation inefficiencies.

In extreme cases, disruptions can lead to long-term or permanent loss of business. Following a large fire in a Philips Electronics manufacturing facility, Ericsson's inability to adapt its supply chain quickly for mobile phone components contributed to the firm's loss of significant market share to competitor Nokia (Sheffi, 2005).

These private-sector effects can spill over into the public sector as well. Business disruptions can lead to significant loss of revenue for local and state governments. The pooled effects of destruction of private infrastructure along with public infrastructure can lead to significant loss of public services, such as freight and public transportation. These public-sector effects were most recently demonstrated by the devastation wrought by Hurricane Katrina. Loss of population and business prompted initial projections of a budget shortfall of as much as $1 billion for the state government of Louisiana[2] and freight transportation was disrupted for months by damage to rail, road ($3 billion [Burton and Hicks, 2005]), and port facilities ($1.7 billion [Blanco, 2005] in Louisiana alone).

Economic and Intangible Consequences of Responding to Terrorism
The unfolding of events and reactions following a terrorist attack can result in a cascade of secondary consequences. In addition to the direct costs of emergency response to the attack, subsequent changes in the nation's posture toward terrorism and the economic impact of those changes can also be construed as consequences of terrorism. Experience from the events of September 11, 2001, strongly suggest that terrorist events will be followed by increased public- and private-sector security investments or increases in insurance rates as firms and the public sector react to new perceived and realized threats (Zycher, 2003).

Terrorism-induced changes in risk perception may also lead individuals and firms to change their consumption and investment preferences. Some business sectors might experience loss of future revenue. This could be particularly significant for luxury and substitutable industries, such as jewelry or travel tourism, respectively.

Large terrorist events might also provoke shifts in foreign policy and have domestic political consequences. By analogy to the costs of the Iraq war, Linda Bilmes and Joseph Stiglitz (2006) have suggested that costs from shifting political focus might compound other human and economic consequences of the Iraq war, thereby contributing to

---

[2]   Hochberg (2005). Note that apparent increases in sales tax receipts from increased purchases ultimately eased the projected deficits.

reduced confidence in the national economy, and ultimately leading to the macroeconomic effect of decreased foreign investment. This kind of effect could alter even technological innovation, if severe uncertainty about the future were to lead to a reduced tolerance for risk investments. These kinds of effects could lead to shifts and loss of value in domestic securities markets.

Though these consequences are poorly understood and difficult to estimate, it is prudent to consider proactively how they may arise and how alternative responses might amplify or counter them. Scenario-based tools, such as day-after gaming, may be particularly useful for assessing risk management for these types of consequences.

Methods of Estimating Consequences of Maritime Terrorism

Past maritime terrorist events provide the most direct means of estimating the consequences of future attacks. However, there are two significant limitations to relying on this type of historical analysis. First, terrorist attacks on maritime targets are fortunately infrequent. As discussed in Chapter Two, a few events can be used as benchmarks for the potential consequences of terrorist attacks. However, the small number of events is limiting because it does not provide a representative sample of attack modes that terrorism analysts have discussed. Second, historical analysis does not provide a means for extrapolating to events that may occur as terrorists adapt and affect maritime systems in new ways.

Therefore, additional approaches are necessary to augment this direct historical analysis. In the analysis of risks of cruise, passenger, and container ships in the subsequent chapters, we used three additional sources of information.

First, terrorist attacks in nonmaritime arenas can provide a measure of typical fatalities and injuries from different attack modes. While maritime attacks are relatively rare, terrorists have been active with land-based and aviation-based attacks for decades. Reviewing shootings, suicide bombings in crowds, and hijackings in other scenarios can provide a better understanding of what the consequences of these attacks might be in the maritime domain.

Second, modeling and simulation can provide estimates of direct and indirect impacts of terrorism. Physical models have been used to understand the impacts of weapons on structures and humans. These can be used to estimate the casualties from conventional, nuclear, radiological, and biological weapons. Direct economic effects can often be easily estimated through modeling and simulation, though uncertainty in the extent of disruptions must be addressed. Economic models, such as input-output models, represent the interdependencies of sectors in the economy. Day-after games and scenario analysis can be used to elicit expert estimates of consequences and how firms and individuals will respond to terrorist events. All of these tools can be used to estimate the indirect effects of terrorism on regional and national economies.

Finally, non–terrorist-related events that cause disruptions provide additional proxies for infrastructure disruptions that might occur following terrorist attacks.[3] Natural disasters like the Northridge Earthquake, Hurricane Andrew, and Hurricane Katrina provide case studies of large-scale regional disruption. Labor disputes like the 2002 West Coast port lockout provide another source of case studies that can be used as a proxy for disruptions.

---

[3]   Although natural disasters (for example) can provide useful proxies for the infrastructure disruptions that might follow from terrorist attacks, disasters are not a good proxy for the civil liability consequences of attacks, because attacks are unique in that they involve the independent criminal actions of terrorists. We discuss the tort liability implications of this distinction in Chapter Four of this book.

Civil Liability and Maritime Terrorism

One of the defining hallmarks of a terrorist attack is that it inflicts damage and harm on persons and property, usually outside the context of conventional warfare. The victims of terrorist aggression are frequently private citizens and commercial interests, for whom the central problem in the wake of a terrorist attack is recovering from the damages inflicted and, where possible, seeking compensation for those damages from any available resource. In the ordinary course of the U.S. civil justice system, deliberate injuries inflicted by one person or group on another are frequently tortious. Such injuries offer a basis for filing a lawsuit to recover damages. Terrorism, however, presents problems for this sort of conventional tort recovery. Lawsuits filed by victims against terrorist perpetrators can be difficult to pursue, particularly when perpetrators deliberately kill themselves to perpetrate an attack, or when perpetrators are international fugitives who are impossible to locate or to investigate.[1] Lawsuits filed against state sponsors of terrorism also present major challenges. One such challenge lies in developing the evidence to tie responsibility for terrorist acts to foreign governments. A second involves overcoming traditional legal rules that, until recently, protected sovereign states from civil suits brought by U.S. nationals in U.S. courts.[2] As a result, victims of terrorist attacks that occur within

---

[1] Even where such lawsuits are legally practical, they may nevertheless be financially nonviable: Individual terrorists and terrorist groups may lack the financial resources to make tort litigation against them worthwhile. See Dellapenna (1996, p. 14).

[2] For discussion of the historical difficulties associated with pursuing U.S. civil litigation against state sponsors of terrorism, see Dellapenna (1996). Note, however, that U.S. legisla-

U.S. territory may be compelled to look beyond perpetrators in seeking compensation for their injuries through the justice system. When terrorists target high-profile U.S. assets and transit systems (as on September 11), the custodians and owners of those systems will themselves become defendants in civil litigation, on the theory that those parties have a duty to prevent, or to mitigate the effects of, terrorist attacks.

Civil liability is an important dimension to consider in examining the impact of maritime terrorist threats on the United States. Liability is tied not only to the harms actually inflicted by an attack, but also to complicated legal rules that shift associated costs from one party to another. To the extent that U.S. law makes commercial shippers, ports, and vessel owners responsible for terrorist attacks that strike at their own operations, those parties will become a focus for redistributing a significant, and possibly catastrophic, set of terrorism risks. In the wake of an actual terrorist event, the costs of civil liability to such parties could become enormous. Yet quantifying the magnitude of liability risk in connection with terrorist attacks remains difficult, because tort principles associated with such attacks are not fully settled under U.S. law.[3] Liability problems associated with *maritime* terrorism are especially complicated. This is true for several reasons. First, maritime commerce often involves intricate relationships between multiple business entities that may share responsibility for shipping operations and that owe contractual obligations to each other. How terrorism liability risk is actually apportioned among these parties in connection with a particular attack involves detailed questions both of fact and of

---

tive reforms in 1996 ameliorated some of the legal problems associated with these sorts of civil claims, particularly by revising the Foreign Intelligence Surveillance Act (FISA) to create an exception to immunity for state sponsors of terrorism. The 1996 FISA reforms eventually culminated in a multibillion-dollar settlement with the government of Libya on behalf of the victims of the Pan Am 103 Lockerbie bombing. See discussion in Skinner (2004). Despite the fact that U.S. law is now more receptive to civil claims against state sponsors of terrorism, the practical challenges associated with such claims remain formidable.

[3] Note that although it is easy to imagine hypothetical terrorist attacks that look superficially similar to maritime accidents (e.g., explosions on board ships), the liability dimension of these two types of events is very different, because liability for terrorism involves holding firms responsible for the independent acts of terrorists. For this reason, liability principles and incentives relating to accidents provide little insight with regard to terrorism.

law. Second, U.S. maritime activities are generally subject to admiralty jurisdiction and to a special set of federal admiralty laws that establish some unique liability rules and legal standards in regard to certain kinds of maritime torts and settings. Finally, liability problems in maritime terrorism are complex partly because potential attack scenarios are broadly varied and fundamentally heterogeneous, in ways that may be tied to basic legal questions about U.S. jurisdiction and choice of law. Related scenarios range from small-scale attacks on domestic passenger shipping[4] to catastrophic attacks involving concealed weapons of mass destruction entering the United States through seaports. Even if U.S. terrorism liability rules were static and unambiguous, the application of those rules to widely disparate maritime terrorism scenarios presents an element of considerable legal uncertainty.

For policymakers seeking to manage maritime terrorism liability and risk, the threshold challenge is to avoid becoming overwhelmed by a labyrinth of jurisdictional issues, legal rules, attack scenarios, and commercial relationships. In the analysis that follows, we endeavor to provide a basic framework for thinking about civil liability in the context of maritime terrorist events in the United States (see Figure 4.1). We highlight some key aspects of U.S. maritime law that are likely to influence future civil litigation over attacks, and we discuss how those laws might apply to different sorts of attacks. We distinguish between tort liability and contractual liability that might arise as a result of future terrorist events, and we describe why the former may present more difficulty and more ambiguity than the latter. We identify a central problem in legal doctrine regarding third-party tort liability for harms caused by terrorist attacks, and we discuss the implications of that doctrine for the commercial parties and interests who may assume tort liability as a result of it. In the end, our analysis does not specify the scope of terrorism liability risk for parties in maritime commerce, because current U.S. law is neither clear nor uniform in defining the boundaries of such liability. Instead, we offer some observations regarding key points in the law and legal issues that could offer a focus for

---

4 For example, a small-scale attack could involve a limited highjacking incident resulting in a single fatality and no property damage; compare this to the *Achille Lauro* incident.

Figure 4.1
Summary Flowchart on Liability Problems in Maritime Terrorism

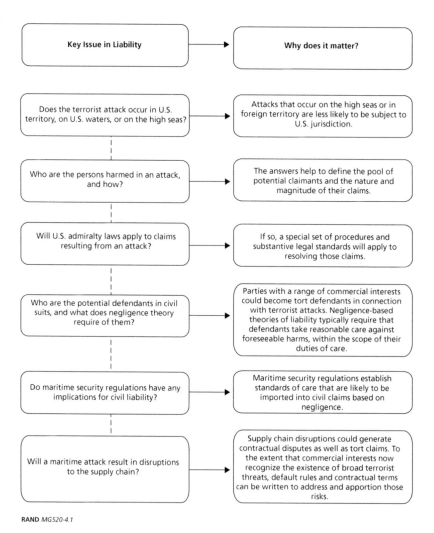

Key Issue in Liability	Why does it matter?
Does the terrorist attack occur in U.S. territory, on U.S. waters, or on the high seas?	Attacks that occur on the high seas or in foreign territory are less likely to be subject to U.S. jurisdiction.
Who are the persons harmed in an attack, and how?	The answers help to define the pool of potential claimants and the nature and magnitude of their claims.
Will U.S. admiralty laws apply to claims resulting from an attack?	If so, a special set of procedures and substantive legal standards will apply to resolving those claims.
Who are the potential defendants in civil suits, and what does negligence theory require of them?	Parties with a range of commercial interests could become tort defendants in connection with terrorist attacks. Negligence-based theories of liability typically require that defendants take reasonable care against foreseeable harms, within the scope of their duties of care.
Do maritime security regulations have any implications for civil liability?	Maritime security regulations establish standards of care that are likely to be imported into civil claims based on negligence.
Will a maritime attack result in disruptions to the supply chain?	Supply chain disruptions could generate contractual disputes as well as tort claims. To the extent that commercial interests now recognize the existence of broad terrorist threats, default rules and contractual terms can be written to address and apportion those risks.

RAND *MG520-4.1*

future reforms by policymakers. We conclude with a brief examination of (1) the relationship between liability rules and insurance practices and (2) the implications of terrorism risk for maritime insurance and commerce more generally. Participants in maritime commerce confront the problem of how to manage their terrorism risks, in light of evolving liability rules. Government officials confront a somewhat different problem: to decide the extent to which civil liability principles *should* apply to terrorism risks, or are instead fundamentally ill-suited to address them.

Bounding the Scope of Civil Liability: U.S. Territory Versus International Waters

The defining hallmark of a *maritime* terrorism scenario involves some connection between a hypothetical attack and navigable waterways. As described in Chapter Two, related events could include attacks on shipping, on seaports, or on shoreside facilities, or attacks that employ cargo containers in order to inflict harm at an inland location. As a threshold matter, some terrorist attacks on passenger and containerized shipping fall entirely outside the jurisdictional bounds of U.S. legal authority and are unlikely to be subject to U.S. civil liability rules. An obvious example might be a terrorist attack on a foreign passenger vessel (e.g., a ferry), occurring in the internal waters of a foreign state (e.g., an inland waterway), and without any involvement by U.S. nationals as passengers or crew. In general, a terrorist attack that has no connection to the United States whatsoever would not be subject to U.S. laws or jurisdiction. It would instead be addressed through the legal rules and authority of the sovereign state in which the attack takes place.[5] Our inquiry here focuses on examining U.S. civil liability issues, for those maritime terrorist events where U.S. laws and jurisdiction are most likely to apply. Setting aside hypothetical attacks that occur either clearly within

---

[5]   Note, however, that even an overseas attack with no direct connection to the United States could still have secondary effects on U.S. citizens that might lead to civil liability issues. For example, though an attack on a foreign ferry might have no direct connection to the United States, one could imagine a ferry owned through a series of corporate parents and ultimately by shareholders in a public company or investment fund that is registered in the United States. Thus, in the wake of a maritime terrorist attack, one could imagine the possibility for secondary lawsuits filed by U.S. shareholders on claims of violations of the disclosure standards embedded in U.S. securities laws. Here again, though, these sorts of lawsuits involve a somewhat peripheral set of liability issues and, in any event, are likely to depend on how the direct victims of an attack are compensated under applicable foreign law.

U.S. territory and waters (where U.S. law applies) or clearly within foreign territory and waters (where U.S. law is unlikely to apply), a third category of potential attack scenarios remains in which the relevance of U.S. law is considerably more ambiguous: What are the limits of application for U.S. jurisdiction and civil liability concerning terrorist attacks on passenger vessels on the high seas?[6]

The answer to this question draws partly on international treaties and common law doctrines concerning jurisdiction on the high seas generally and, in particular, in relation to acts of piracy and terrorism. The general rule regarding police and judicial jurisdiction on the high seas is (1) that it cannot be arbitrarily imposed by a state on a foreign-flagged vessel and (2) that the flag state ordinarily retains sole jurisdiction and regulatory authority over its own flagged vessels while they operate on the high seas.[7] The 1982 United Nations Convention on the Law of the Sea (UNCLOS) clarifies that foreign-flagged vessels only become subject to the jurisdiction of a state when operating within that state's territorial waters.[8] Perhaps the most important exception to the general rule regarding jurisdiction on the high seas involves acts of piracy, which, pursuant to UNCLOS and international common law, can become subject to the jurisdiction of any state, regardless of the flag status of a pirated vessel, because piratical acts have customarily been viewed as "crimes against the human race" (Jesus, 2003, p. 374). Notwithstanding this expansive rule on jurisdiction over piracy, however, jurisdiction over terrorism on the high seas is likely to be somewhat

---

[6]   As a practical matter, note that maritime terrorist attacks occurring on the high seas are arguably more likely to target passenger vessels than containerized cargo vessels, since cargo containers are primarily attractive as a mode of conveyance rather than as a terrorist target per se. Thus, the most ambiguous attack scenarios with regard to the application of U.S. jurisdiction and admiralty laws are likely to involve terrorist hijackings of, or attacks upon, foreign-flagged passenger liners operating outside U.S. territorial waters, but with U.S. passengers on board.

[7]   See commentary in Jesus (2003, p. 373), Garmon (2002, p. 268), and Wing (2003, p. 174). See also generally Halberstam (1988), Diaz and Dubner (2004), and Mellor (2002).

[8]   See Wing (2003, p. 179) and United Nations (1982, p. 58, Article 92). See also Schulkin (2002, p. 120).

more limited. In particular, UNCLOS defines piracy as acts involving violence, detention, or depredation committed "for private ends" (United Nations, 1982, pp. 60–61). Commentators have disputed for years exactly what "private ends" means, but the consensus appears to distinguish terrorist acts (i.e., those politically motivated) from piratical acts (i.e., those criminally motivated), with the former falling outside the rule of universal jurisdiction.[9] Subsequent international treaty efforts designed to combat maritime terrorism have created separate legal grounds and mechanisms for international jurisdiction over high-seas terrorist attacks, but with rules that could easily create conflicting or ambiguous jurisdiction among multiple sovereign states under some circumstances.[10] Whether any of these international treaty grounds for high-seas jurisdiction would apply in the context of a tort claim against a third-party defendant is less than clear. It will likely depend on the facts of a particular attack.[11]

In sum, all maritime terrorism scenarios can be grouped into one of three categories. Attacks occurring in U.S. territory or waters clearly fall into U.S. jurisdiction and would be dealt with through U.S. civil liability rules. Our discussion of liability focuses implicitly on this set

---

[9]   See discussion in Jesus (2003, pp. 377–379), Garmon (2002, p. 265), and Halberstam (1988, pp. 272–291).

[10]   See generally United Nations (1988), and commentary by Mellor (2002, pp. 382–386). Note that the Convention for Suppression of Unlawful Acts Against the Safety of Maritime Navigation (SUA) creates mandatory jurisdiction for the flag state, for the territorial state (i.e., when an unlawful maritime act is committed within a state's territorial waters), and for the state of nationality of the perpetrator of the unlawful act. In addition, a state is also permitted to establish jurisdiction under SUA when the victims of an offense are nationals of that state, when an offense is designed to coerce that state into a particular action, or when the perpetrator is a stateless person whose habitual residence is in that state. See United Nations (1988, Article 6).

[11]   Note also that even when the United States can exert jurisdiction over terrorist events that occur on the high seas, it does not necessarily follow that U.S. substantive law applies to questions related to third-party liability. U.S. common law includes several precedents dealing with international choice-of-law issues in admiralty cases, which, in determining the appropriate legal rules to apply in a particular case, require an inquiry into multiple factors, including the place of the wrongful act, the law of the flag state, the allegiance of the injured party and of the defendant shipowner, and the law of the forum state. See discussion in Force (2004, pp. 22–23).

of attack scenarios. By contrast, attacks occurring in foreign territorial waters would ordinarily not fall under U.S. jurisdiction and, depending on the facts involved in a particular case, most aspects of civil liability would likely be resolved under foreign substantive laws. Finally, terrorist attacks on the high seas present ambiguity in terms of the extent to which U.S. jurisdiction and civil liability rules would apply. While U.S. admiralty law and international conventions both appear to create grounds for U.S. jurisdiction in connection with high seas terrorist attacks, exactly how such jurisdiction might apply to specific third-party liability claims is not clear under the law and would likely depend on the facts in a specific case.

Civil Liability Analysis Always Begins by Identifying Who Is Hurt

Hypothetical maritime terrorist attacks could involve direct and indirect harms to a large number of persons and businesses. Particularly in the event of a catastrophic attack, the harms could be widespread; they also might result in an abundance of tort theories for recovery. It is not difficult to imagine scenarios that could involve hundreds or thousands of persons seeking compensation for the negligent infliction of emotional distress, to imagine physically distant business interests seeking compensation for foreseeable economic disruptions, to imagine large-scale environmental liability problems that might emerge from an attack, or to imagine stockholders in an affected public company seeking damages from directors and officers on theories of breach fiduciary duty or of failure to disclose risks adequately. These kinds of scenarios can rapidly spiral into very technical analyses of liability rules that might apply to specific cases. But they obscure a more general principle for understanding and evaluating liability problems in connection with maritime terrorist attacks. The impact of civil liability rules is not to create harm, but rather to transfer related costs from one party to another.[12] Thus, the injuries that people and property owners actually suffer as the result of an attack ultimately bound the scope of liability. Identifying the categories of persons and business interests directly harmed is always the first step in understanding liability problems associated with terrorism, because those persons and interests will become the primary plaintiffs in any civil suits to recover damages.

Consider the application of this principle to maritime terrorism scenarios involving attacks on passenger shipping. Who is likely to be harmed in the context of such attacks, and how?[13] Clearly, the primary effect of attacks on ferries or on cruise liners is the potential for human casualties among passengers and crew members. Related harms are not limited to deaths: They could potentially extend to other sorts of physical injuries and emotional trauma as well, plus secondary types of injuries, such as loss of consortium. The other obvious potential effect from attacks on ferries or cruise liners is harm to property, which, in the most straightforward cases, would presumably take the form of damage to, or destruction of, a target ship. Assuming that this captures the kinds of injuries that are likely to result from attacks on passenger shipping, it also describes the potential plaintiffs and the kinds of tort claims that they are most likely to assert. Even for the most egregious terrorist attacks on passenger ships, i.e., those designed to maximize casualties and the loss of life, the magnitude and nature of potential civil liability can still be understood within this simple framework. More-exotic terrorism scenarios involving passenger shipping could conceivably involve additional categories of injuries and the possibil-

---

[12] Note, however, that transfer payments made under the civil justice system involve high transaction costs, as estimated by past empirical studies. See, e.g., Tillinghast-Towers Perrin (2004). Apart from any other considerations regarding the operation of the civil justice system in compensating terrorism victims, the justice system is clearly expensive to administer.

[13] See also Chapter Three in regard to defining the consequences of maritime terrorist attacks more broadly. Note that the questions of who is likely to be harmed and how involve a narrow focus on physical harms to people and property and on other forms of damage immediately connected to those physical harms. Some of the broader effects of terrorism (e.g., in degrading public infrastructure and institutions, inflicting general economic disruption, or in shifting U.S. foreign policy) fall outside the scope of liability analysis, because either (1) these effects are not traditionally compensable in tort or (2) the associated harms may be nebulous and impossible to quantify.

ity for physical harms to persons or property beyond a single, targeted ship. But even in those sorts of scenarios, the initial analysis of liability depends on the following:

- identifying the injuries and damages that are likely to result from an attack
- the identity and likely claims of potential plaintiffs (see Table 4.1).

Terrorist attacks involving container shipping present a more complicated set of problems for this kind of threshold liability analysis. Again, the primary harms inflicted in these sorts of scenarios will involve human injuries, deaths, and damage to property. But because

Table 4.1
Direct Harms and Liability in Two Categories of Maritime Terrorism

Harm	Attacks on Passenger Shipping	Attacks on Container Shipping
Physical harm to victims	Focus of attacks on passenger shipping is harm to passengers and crew. Physical harm to persons beyond a target ship is less likely.	Depending on the nature of attack, physical harm to victims could be either nonexistent or very widespread. Victims could potentially be far removed from the maritime setting.
Damage to property	Less focal. For most scenarios, property damage would be limited to the target ship or to the personal property of passengers on board the ship.	Damage to property is a logical aim for attacks on container shipping. Such damage could target ships, seaports, containerized cargo, or other facilities and property in proximity to shipping containers.
Business disruption	Less focal. For most scenarios involving attacks in the United States, business disruption would be limited to the commercial owner of a targeted ship or to passenger shipping and tourism more generally, but with only limited disruptions to broader commerce.[a]	Supply chain disruption is a logical aim for attacks on container shipping. Damage to property or port facilities could have direct effects on downstream commercial interests, and closure of seaports or shipping lanes could have widespread disruptive effects on U.S. commerce.

[a] Note, however, that business disruption effects related to terrorist attacks on passenger shipping are geographically contextual and, in the case of at least some international "choke points," e.g., a hypothetical attack on ferry traffic across the English channel, broad-based business disruption effects could plausibly occur.

the spectrum of potential terrorist attacks involving container shipping is broader and more heterogeneous, so, too, is the pool of potential victims. Persons physically harmed in a terrorist attack involving containerized shipping could include crew members and seaport workers, but because shipping containers are attractive to terrorists primarily as a method of conveyance rather than as a target, attacks delivered via container could likely be aimed at persons unconnected with maritime industry. Notably, attacks involving concealed chemical, biological, radiological, or nuclear (CBRN) weapons could plausibly inflict mass casualties and, in some scenarios, might result in toxic exposure for large numbers of persons, with risks for subsequent development of long-term illness.[14] Physical harm to property in attacks involving containerized shipping could take on many forms as well, ranging from direct damage to containerized sea vessels to the destruction of property interests entirely removed from maritime activity (apart from proximity to cargo containers). Despite the heterogeneity, the threshold step in evaluating related liability issues remains the same as in the passenger shipping scenarios. The initial questions that bound liability are who is likely to be harmed in a hypothetical attack and how (see Table 4.1). Attacks involving containerized shipping add another category of direct harms beyond physical injuries and property losses, in the form of potential disruptions to the supply chain. When the results of a terrorist attack break a chain of commercial transactions (e.g., as between suppliers and manufacturers), the result could be to disrupt the operations of business interests far removed from the physical site of an attack. We discuss some of the liability implications of maritime supply chain disruptions in more detail later in this chapter. For current purposes, it suffices to note that this is another category of harm that enters into the calculus of liability.

---

[14] Widespread toxic exposures in the context of a terrorist attack could create an additional set of civil liability complexities, akin to those involved in mass toxic torts like asbestos and agent orange. Many other researchers have examined liability problems and litigation patterns in connection with toxic torts (see, e.g., Carroll et al., 2005). For current purposes, it suffices to recognize that terrorism-related toxic exposures could juxtapose an additional set of legal complexities onto those associated with third-party tort liability for terrorist acts more generally.

The reason for framing the analysis of civil liability in terms of who gets hurt and how is to simplify and organize related legal problems associated with maritime terrorism. In the event of a significant maritime attack, many additional parties could experience indirect injuries as a result. But the technical legalities of civil suits for secondary or indirect harms are likely to be subordinate to the merits of more central liability claims brought by persons who are directly injured in an attack. For example, some commentators have discussed the potential for terrorism-associated liability on the part of corporate officers and directors, in connection either with a breach of their fiduciary duties or with a failure to disclose terrorism risks adequately to their shareholders.[15] The merits of these kinds of liability suits are not well-resolved under current law. What is clear, though, is that the scope and validity of these sorts of claims will likely depend, at least in part, on how the civil justice system handles the claims of the direct victims of a terrorist attack. To the extent that the law upholds third-party tort claims filed by persons directly harmed in a terrorist attack, then the companies that bear liability as a result will also be placed at risk for derivative civil suits brought by their own shareholders. To the extent that the law rejects the tort claims of persons directly harmed by a terrorist attack, then the potential for secondary shareholder derivative suits appears substantially diminished.

The application of civil liability rules to particular terrorism scenarios involves complicated questions of fact and of law and areas of legal doctrine not fully settled. The threshold challenge for policymakers in understanding liability is to gauge who is likely to be harmed in a terrorist attack and what the nature of that harm is likely to look like. By corollary, answers to those questions will identify the most important categories of plaintiffs for potential litigation. The answers will also characterize the sorts of civil claims that those plaintiffs might seek to bring. Potential liability in specific maritime terrorism scenarios is bounded by an analysis of the harms that the terrorists would likely inflict. Such an analysis then frames the legal rules that would determine the outcome of civil claims and thereby the transfer of related

---

[15] See, e.g., discussion in Cunningham (2004).

costs from direct victims in an attack to third parties with responsibility to prevent or to mitigate an attack.

U.S. Admiralty Law and Its Application to Maritime Terrorist Attacks

One of the unique aspects of U.S. law concerning maritime activities and commerce is a special set of procedural and substantive rules in admiralty. Under the U.S. Constitution, federal courts have subject-matter jurisdiction over maritime and admiralty matters.[16] This is important partly because it means that plaintiffs in admiralty disputes are automatically entitled to bring their claims in federal court and because federal admiralty laws, as opposed to state laws, may apply to the resolution of those claims. U.S. admiralty jurisdiction in tort cases requires an allegation that the tort occurred on navigable waters and that the tort bears some nexus to traditional maritime activities.[17] By contrast, admiralty jurisdiction in contract cases involves an analysis of the subject matter of a disputed contract, which must be characterized as "maritime" pursuant to a series of U.S. common law precedents.[18] The contours of admiralty jurisdiction are likely to affect the analysis of civil liability problems in connection with specific maritime terrorist threats against the United States. For example, admiralty jurisdiction carries with it special procedural rules and choices for plaintiffs, most notably in regard to whether to bring an admiralty claim in state or

---

[16] See discussion in Force (2004, p. 1); see also *The Constitution of the United States of America* (2002, pp. 15–16, Article III) and 28 USC 1333 (1949). See also discussion in Rue (2005, p. 1127).

[17] See Force (2004, p. 5) and Rue (2005, pp. 1129–1130). The implication is that most maritime terrorist attacks involving vessels in navigable U.S. waters would be subject to admiralty jurisdiction, but also that some terrorist attacks on vessels on inland waterways or on other inland targets by means of sabotaged cargo containers, might not.

[18] See discussion in Force (2004, pp. 9–11), Rue (2005, pp. 1130–1133), Gruendel and Crain (2003, pp. 1242–1243). The rules for what does and does not constitute a "maritime" contract for purposes of admiralty jurisdiction are sometimes counterintuitive. For example, a contract for carriage of goods by sea is a maritime contract, while a contract for the building of a vessel is not. See Force (2004, p. 10).

in federal court, which, in turn, could determine whether a plaintiff is entitled to a jury trial.[19] Without examining these sorts of procedural issues in detail, we simply note that they are likely to influence the course of civil litigation in the wake of a maritime terrorist event.[20] More important for current purposes is the existence of a set of federal admiralty laws that could apply in determining third-party civil liability in connection with many maritime terrorism scenarios. These

Table 4.2
Selected Admiralty Laws Relevant to Terrorism Liability

Admiralty Statute	Description
Jones Act (46 USCS Appx 688)	Provides seamen the right to recover from employers for negligence resulting in personal injury or death.
Longshore and Harbor Workers' Compensation Act (LHWCA) (33 USCS 901)	Provides workers' compensation–type benefits for employment-related injuries to harbor workers.
Death on the High Seas Act (DOHSA) (46 USCS Appx 761)	Establishes a basis for wrongful death tort claims for passengers occurring more than three miles from U.S. shores.
Harter Act (46 USCS Appx 190)	Establishes standards of care and immunities for cargo carriers operating in transit between U.S. ports.
Carriage of Goods by Sea Act (COGSA) (46 USCS Appx 1300)	Establishes standards of care and immunities for cargo carriers operating in transit between foreign and U.S. ports.
Limitation of Vessel Owner's Liability Act (LVOLA) (46 USCS Appx 181)	Permits vessel owners to limit their liability in connection with maritime casualties, provided that owner has no "knowledge or privity" connected with the loss.

---

[19] Under the federal "saving to suitors" clause, plaintiffs retain rights to "all other remedies to which they are otherwise entitled" 28 USC 1333. In practice, this means that plaintiffs may pursue common law or other available statutory remedies through state courts. See Force (2004, p. 18).

[20] See Force (2004, pp. 27–39) for a summary of some of the special procedural rules that apply to admiralty cases.

federal maritime rules are different from the liability rules that might otherwise apply on land. We discuss several of the most important aspects of these rules below (see also Table 4.2).

One of the major categories of injury in connection with potential terrorist attacks on U.S. shipping, and particularly on U.S. passenger shipping, involves deaths and injuries to crew and to passengers. On land, a host of legal mechanisms and theories exist to compensate the victims of similar sorts of injuries, ranging from possible tort claims for negligence and wrongful death, to workers' compensation claims for those whose harms are sustained within the course and scope of their employment. The rights and remedies that are available to vessel crew members and passengers in the context of maritime injuries, however, are somewhat unique. Under the federal Jones Act,[21] a seaman possesses the right to recover damages against his or her employer for negligence resulting in personal injury or death.[22] Related claims under the Jones Act turn on detailed legal definitions of who qualifies as a "seaman," what qualifies as a "vessel," and who constitutes an "employer" for purposes of the act.[23] Where a claim under the Jones Act can be made, the seaman (or the seaman's beneficiary) is entitled to a jury trial, and some of the standards for negligence claims that apply under the act are more liberal than those that would typically apply on land.[24] For longshoremen and harbor workers, LHWCA offers a very different set of federal benefits for maritime work-related injuries, with core features simi-

---

[21] 46 USCS Appx 688. See discussion in Force (2004, pp. 91–102); see also Warshauer and Dittman (2005, pp. 1173–1183, 1195–1205).

[22] Note that the Jones Act provides both wrongful death and survival claims for the beneficiaries and dependents of a deceased seaman. See Force (2004, p. 91).

[23] See discussion in Force (2004, pp. 92–96) and Warshauer and Dittman (2005, pp. 1173–1193).

[24] See Force (2004, p. 97). In particular, the Jones Act rules for negligence per se based on statutory violations by an employer do not require that a seaman be within the class of persons that the statute is designed to protect. See Force (2004, p. 97). Note, however, that damages under the Jones Act are limited to pecuniary losses, and do not include other categories of recovery, such as loss of consortium or punitive damages. See Force (2004, p. 120).

lar to those of a workers' compensation statute.[25] And, for passengers who are injured or killed aboard a vessel, several sets of maritime laws provide potential tort remedies. DOHSA provides a basis for wrongful-death tort claims (including those of passengers) that occur more than three miles from U.S. shores (46 USCS Appx 761–768). DOHSA actions can be based on any tort theory and are not limited to negligence claims but, in general, require a showing of proximate causation in order to support a recovery (see Force, 2004, p. 119). Although DOHSA claims do not apply to deaths that occur closer than three miles from shore, several maritime law precedents have established a basis for similar wrongful death claims in such cases.[26] Even more generally, ship owners have a duty under maritime law to exercise reasonable care toward persons lawfully present on their vessels—a basis for negligence claims by passengers in connection with injuries other than death (see Force, 2004, pp. 114–115).

Federal maritime rules also include provisions governing potential tort liability in connection with damage to cargo aboard container shipping vessels and in connection with vessel collisions and allisions.[27] Transportation of goods by water among U.S. ports and between foreign ports and the United States is governed by the Harter Act (46 USCS Appx 190–196) and by COGSA (46 USCS Appx 1300–1315), respectively. The Harter Act prohibits carriers from exculpating themselves from negligence liability for damage to cargo through the use of contractual provisions in shipping documents, e.g., as by a contractual term limiting a vessel owner's vicarious liability for the actions of its agents (46 USCS Appx 190, 191). At the same time, where a carrier exercises appropriate care in making a vessel seaworthy and properly staffing and supplying it, the Harter Act also provides the carrier with protection from liability for damage to cargo resulting from any of an enumerated list of events, most notably including "the acts of public

---

[25] 33 USCS 901–948(a). See discussion in Force (2004, pp. 102–110).

[26] *Moragne v. State Marine Lines* (1970), *Norfolk Shipbuilding v. Garris* (2001). See discussion in Force (2004, pp. 120–122).

[27] Note that a collision occurs between two vessels, while an allision occurs when a vessel strikes a stationary object, such as a wharf. See Force (2004, p. 125).

enemies."[28] The effect of the Harter Act is to help institute a standard for negligence in connection with transportation of goods by water between U.S. ports and to prevent carriers from contracting out of related liability. By contrast with the Harter Act, COGSA applies to cargo shipping between foreign ports and those in the United States and establishes a more specific set of statutory rights and responsibilities for carriers and shippers.[29] Under COGSA, a carrier has a set of duties to ensure the seaworthiness of a ship and to take appropriate care in staffing and supplying it, as well as in the proper handling and maintenance of cargo (46 USCS Appx 1303). Like the Harter Act, COGSA prohibits the exculpation of a carrier's duties by contract and, once again, where a carrier has exercised due care, it becomes entitled to a series of statutory immunities against liability for damage to cargo (46 USCS Appx 1304). Notably, COGSA establishes specific immunities in connection both with "acts of war" and "acts of public enemies."[30] Finally, even when a carrier is not immune from liability under COGSA, the statute also limits compensable damages on cargo to $500 per package or per customary freight unit, unless carrier and shipper agree to a higher limit in advance (46 USCS Appx 1304[5]).

A different set of maritime legal rules applies in collision and allision cases, where damage occurs primarily to vessels (passenger- or cargo-carrying) or, in the case of allision, to stationary objects that vessels strike. Under U.S. law, fault in a collision case may arise from negligent practice by navigators, from a violation of applicable rules of navigation or local customs, or from the unseaworthy condition or malfunction of equipment.[31] Although collision liability is often associ-

---

[28] 46 USCS Appx 192. See also discussion in Force (2004, pp. 57–58).

[29] 46 USCS Appx 1303, 1304. See discussion in Force (2004, p. 64).

[30] 46 USCS Appx 1304(2)(e, f). The question whether a terrorist attack constitutes the "act of a public enemy" under COGSA has been a subject of previous analysis and debate. See, e.g., Clyne (2003, pp. 1216–1217). Although there is some ambiguity in the analysis as it might apply to foreign-flagged vessels, there is nevertheless a strong argument that terrorist attacks are necessarily either directed at a flag state (and thus covered by the "public enemy" clause) or piratical with regard to the flag state (and thus potentially still covered by the "public enemy" clause).

[31] See discussion in Force (2004, p. 126).

ated with a navigator's negligence that causes an accident, such liability might also apply in connection with violation of safety standards established by law. Generally under the doctrine of negligence per se, violation of a legal safety standard is grounds for presuming fault against a party (e.g., a carrier), where violation of that standard results in an injury to someone whom the law was intended to protect.[32] Moreover, under the Pennsylvania Rule, a vessel that commits a violation of a legal safety standard bears the burden of proving that the violation could not have caused an accident, in order to avoid the potential for related liability.[33] Taken together, these doctrines may result in collision liability in situations other than those involving negligence in navigation. In particular, the doctrines might also result in liability in connection with some maritime terrorism scenarios (e.g., where a carrier has violated U.S. regulatory requirements intended to prevent or to mitigate terrorist attacks).[34] Damages recoverable under U.S. collision law depend on whether an affected vessel is deemed a partial or total loss. In the former case, damages may include the cost of repair and the loss of vessel earnings during repair, plus incidental costs. In the later case, damages include the fair value of the vessel plus cleanup and incidental costs, but not the value of the loss of vessel earnings.[35] U.S. law typically limits economic damages in collision cases to plaintiffs possessing a proprietary interest in a damaged vessel.[36] Related

---

[32] See generally discussion in Keeton and Prosser (1984, pp. 220–233).

[33] *The Pennsylvania* (1873). See also discussion in Force (2004, p. 126).

[34] Note also that the Pennsylvania Rule has come to have broader application in maritime law than just in collision cases and, in particular, the rule has been also been applied in maritime personal injury cases. See discussion in Carey (2004, p. 308). Thus, the combination of negligence per se and the Pennsylvania Rule could apply in determining liability for a wide range of maritime tort claims related to a potential terrorist attack.

[35] See generally Force (2004, pp. 128–131), for discussion of maritime precedents on determining collision damages.

[36] See discussion of *Robins Dry Dock and Repair Co. v. Flint* (1927) in Force (2004, p. 129).

rules have generally foreclosed recoveries by those with economic losses but without physical harm as a result of a maritime collision.[37]

One additional maritime legal rule could be important in determining civil liability consequences in connection with some maritime terrorist attacks. Under LVOLA (46 USCS Appx 181–189), a vessel owner may elect to limit its liability following a maritime casualty involving vessels, cargo, or people. More specifically, when a vessel owner has no "privity or knowledge" in connection with the circumstances of a maritime casualty, the owner may respond to civil claims filed against it by instituting a proceeding to limit liability (46 USCS Appx 183[a]). Liability under LVOLA is restricted to the value of the owner's interest in its vessel and any pending freight, though when that amount is insufficient to cover the payment of damages "in respect of loss of life or personal injury," then the vessel owner's liability with respect to those damages is increased to a maximum of $420 per ton of the vessel's tonnage (46 USCS Appx 183[b]). A filing by an owner to limit its liability under LVOLA requires that the owner place on deposit an amount equal to its interest in the vessel and pending freight, pursuant to provisions in the Supplemental Rules of Civil Procedure.[38] Limited liability under LVOLA could potentially enter into play across a broad range of maritime terrorist events, whenever tort claims against a vessel owner are likely to be central in postattack litigation.

The admiralty rules and statutes described above are important in understanding the potential liability consequences of maritime terrorism in the United States, because many of these rules could apply in the context of specific terrorist attacks. For example, attacks on U.S. passenger shipping would likely involve passenger injuries or deaths. Those attacks might well involve DOHSA or federal common law claims. Damages related to those claims could be limited under LVOLA, however, at least to the extent that the claims are brought against a defendant vessel owner. By contrast, claims for damage to goods in an attack involving containerized shipping may be harder to make out, given that

---

[37] See discussion of *Louisiana ex rel. Guste v. M/V Testbank* (1985) in Force (2004, p. 130).

[38] See discussion of Federal Rules of Civil Procedure Supplemental Rule F(2) in Force (2004, pp. 133–134).

both COGSA and the Harter Act provide immunity from liability to carriers in connection with the "acts of public enemies," at least to the extent that the carriers take appropriate care in supplying, equipping, and staffing their vessels. Although the application of these admiralty laws to future maritime terrorist events seems almost inevitable, it is less than clear exactly how the statutes (or existing precedents interpreting them) would apply to the facts of hypothetical terrorism cases. In any potential terrorism-related claim against vessel owners or carriers in which negligence or fault is asserted, future questions will arise around the scope of the legal duty that is owed and what the appropriate standard of care specifically requires. Even the limitation of vessel owner liability under LVOLA is contingent on an owner lacking "knowledge" in connection with the circumstances of a maritime casualty: Again, it is not clear how the rule would be interpreted in connection with future terrorist incidents. We discuss the core set of legal ambiguities surrounding terrorism and third-party negligence doctrines in more detail below.

Two additional complications are likely to constrain the influence of federal admiralty laws in fully determining civil liability following a maritime terrorist attack. First, even simple attack scenarios (e.g., a terrorist hijacking of a passenger vessel on the high seas) could involve tort claims against defendants *other* than ship owners and carriers. To the extent that parties on shore and unconnected with a ship contribute to the circumstances that result in an attack, tort liability for those parties might well be subject to legal rules other than those in admiralty. An example might involve a failure by a land-based security company to perform its functions with due care, with the foreseeable result of allowing terrorists or their contraband to penetrate into a harbor facility. Liability for the security company might be predicated on an act of negligence committed by its agents on land, even though the actual damage from the subsequent attack occurs later and on the water. By implication, even a simple terrorist attack could involve multiple civil claims against multiple defendants: Some of those claims will likely be based on admiralty law, but some might not. Second, and on a related point, the contours of federal preemption are far from clear as applied to state laws that might, or might not, encroach on federal admiralty laws. In at least some past instances, state law claims for maritime torts have been upheld against federal preemption (see Force, 2004, pp. 23–26). This means that even where federal admiralty laws clearly apply, plaintiffs may sometimes also have access to additional claims or rights of action under state law. Although past cases have established preemption of state remedies in connection with claims under the Jones Act, DOHSA, LHWCA, and COGSA (Force, 2004, p. 24), future terrorism liability cases could potentially require new analyses on the federal preemption of state laws.

Defendants and Negligence Tort Claims in Maritime Terrorism

If the initial step in analyzing liability in maritime terrorist attacks is to identify the likely plaintiffs and the nature and extent of their probable injuries, then the next step involves identifying the likely defendants and the legal grounds on which they might be sued. Again, the key plaintiffs in a maritime terrorism scenario will be the persons directly harmed by an attack. Potential defendants are somewhat more difficult to identify. In all maritime terrorism scenarios, third-party defendants will be independent of terrorist attackers and will instead be parties whose commercial or property interests somehow become implicated or targeted by the circumstances of an attack. In general, tort claims against these defendants will require that the defendants' conduct be (1) causally connected with the harms suffered by plaintiffs and (2) legally actionable by them. The point is illustrated by civil litigation in the wake of the September 11 attacks, in which consolidated claims have been brought against airlines, airport security companies, airport operators, airplane manufacturers, and the owners and operators of the World Trade Center buildings and businesses (see *In re September 11 Litig.*, 2003, p. 287). Each of these parties was allegedly in a position to help prevent the attacks or to mitigate the consequences. By analogy in a hypothetical maritime terrorist attack, potential defendants could include carriers and ship owners, port facilities, originators of cargo shipments, and manufacturers of vessels or security equipment. Furthermore, in scenarios in which vessels or cargo containers are employed as a means to attack other targets, e.g., inland transshipment facilities, the owners and operators of those land-based facilities could also become defendants in civil litigation. With the exception of potential product liability claims,[39] most of the tort claims against defendants in a maritime terrorist attack would likely involve variations on negligence theory, and the argument that defendants' breached their legal duties of care to the plaintiffs.[40]

Identifying more specifically the civil claims and legal rules that might apply in the context of a hypothetical terrorist attack is highly fact dependent. Different maritime terrorism scenarios could involve very different groups of injured persons, differences in the nature of the injuries and in the pool of potential commercial defendants, and differences in the site of an attack, with potential consequences for both legal jurisdiction and choice of law. For example, a relatively simple maritime terrorism scenario might involve a small-scale attack on a passenger vessel in the United States with damages limited to a single fatality.[41] Assuming the attack occurs on navigable water, then admiralty jurisdiction and maritime legal rules will likely apply to the wrongful death claim.[42] Potential defendants could include the carrier and vessel owner, as well as perhaps the port facility through which terrorists boarded the vessel. Each of these defendants might be subject to

---

[39] Under strict product-liability doctrine, the manufacturer of a product can be held liable for defects in the design or manufacture of a product, without regard to whether the manufacturer breached a duty to exercise reasonable care in conducting its operations. See discussion in Keeton and Prosser (1984, pp. 694–702). Without analyzing all of the doctrinal issues that might arise in maritime product-liability claims related to terrorist attacks, we do note that under the SAFETY Act provisions of the Homeland Security Act of 2002 (6 USCS Appx 101), manufacturers of approved antiterrorism technologies may be entitled to invoke a "government contractor" defense against strict product-liability claims. See 6 USC 442.

[40] See discussion in *In re September 11 Litig.* (2003, p. 288), describing negligence claims against airlines, airport security companies, airport operators, World Trade Center owners and operators, Port Authority of New York and New Jersey, and Boeing.

[41] Compare with *Achille Lauro* incident.

[42] See earlier discussion of U.S. admiralty law. Note, however, that the plaintiff in this case might have access to additional claims under state law and that federal preemption rules regarding such claims are not entirely clear. See discussion in Force (2004, pp. 120–122).

negligence-based tort claims. At the other extreme, a high-impact maritime terrorism scenario could plausibly involve the use of a containerized cargo shipment to execute a CBRN attack at an inland site in the United States. Depending on where the actual attack occurs (e.g., on water or on land), civil claims connected to mass casualties and catastrophic property losses might or might not invoke U.S. maritime laws. Moreover, given that a sabotaged cargo container could easily pass through the hands of multiple carriers, ports, and commercial parties, possibly both in the United States and abroad, then the alleged torts of each of the defendants might likely have occurred in a different jurisdiction. Determining exactly which legal rules would apply in evaluating the conduct of each defendant in this sort of scenario could require a nontrivial choice-of-law analysis.[43]

Regardless of the specific substantive laws that would apply to resolving negligence-based claims in connection with a maritime terrorist attack, two core legal issues would need to be resolved in any such claim. First is the question whether the defendants in a maritime terrorism case owe *any* recognized duty of care to the plaintiffs, given that U.S. common law has traditionally been conservative in imposing liability on defendants for their failure to control the conduct of others, particularly where that conduct is criminal.[44] In a relatively recent analysis of this issue, the court in the September 11 litigation addressed the question under New York law and applied a balancing test of several factors, including "the reasonable expectations of parties and society generally, the proliferation of claims, the likelihood of unlimited or insurer-like liability, disproportionate risk and reparation

---

[43] Note that in the case of litigation arising out of the September 11 attacks, Congress simplified the choice-of-law problem through relevant provisions of the Air Transportation Safety and System Stabilization Act (ATSSSA) (49 USC 40101). ATSSSA established exclusive jurisdiction for civil claims related to the attacks in the U.S. District Court for the Southern District of New York and further established that the applicable substantive law for all claims would be derived from the rules of the state in which each crash occurred. In the event of a future maritime terrorist attack involving mass casualties or destruction, Congress might well intervene again to simplify jurisdictional and choice-of-law issues.

[44] See *In re September 11 Litig.* (2003, p. 290); see also Keeton and Prosser (1984, pp. 201–203).

allocation, and public policies affecting the expansion or limitation of new channels of liability."[45] Based on that balancing test, the court concluded that the September 11 defendants *did* owe duties of care to the plaintiffs (see *In re September 11 Litig.*, 2003, pp. 290–295). A second and related legal question arises in defining the scope of the duty that defendants have to safeguard plaintiffs, particularly in connection with terrorist attacks. Traditionally, the scope of duty in most negligence cases is tied to the concept of *foreseeability*: Defendants have a duty to take reasonable precautions against foreseeable risks. By corollary, defendants do not have a duty to protect against risks they cannot foresee, nor can their conduct be viewed as having caused unforeseeable injuries.[46] Again, legal questions about the foreseeability of terrorist attacks were addressed in a preliminary decision in the September 11 litigation, with a ruling that favored the plaintiffs and concluded that their claims could not be thrown out based on the putative lack of foreseeability of the terrorist attacks (see *In re September 11 Litig.*, 2003, pp. 295–297).

For purposes of evaluating future civil claims in connection with maritime terrorism, several broad implications emerge. Defendants against such claims will likely include all of the commercial parties whose operations or property interests are directly targeted or touched by an attack and who arguably might have been able to prevent or to mitigate it through their own conduct. Tort claims against the defendants will likely include many variations on negligence theory and perhaps on strict product-liability theory as well, though the particular legal standards that apply in any given case will depend heavily on the facts of that case. More specifically, although U.S. maritime laws could apply to resolve many related claims in many hypothetical attack scenarios, other state and federal laws could potentially apply to claims asserting negligent security practices or precautions based on land.

---

[45] See *Palka v. Servicemaster Management Servs. Corp.* (1994); see also *In re September 11 Litig.* (2003, p. 290).

[46] Negligence liability for the criminal acts of third parties has traditionally been quite limited, in large part because such activities were viewed as unforeseeable in most circumstances. See discussion and examples in Keeton and Prosser (1984, pp. 201–203). See also discussion in Reynolds (1996) and Gash (2002–2003, pp. 601–603).

Perhaps most importantly, any future negligence claims connected with maritime terrorism will confront fundamental questions about whether defendants owe any legal duties to plaintiffs and whether specific maritime terrorist attacks are foreseeable for purposes of determining negligent misconduct. Preliminary rulings in the September 11 litigation have favored plaintiffs on these issues, and suggest that courts might interpret legal theories of duty and foreseeability liberally in the future (see *In re September 11 Litig.*, 2003, pp. 295–297). If so, third-party tort liability for maritime terrorist attacks is likely to become expansive. Given that the experience of September 11 has now placed both the public and maritime interests on notice for the risk of terrorist threats not previously recognized or well-understood, the scope of "foreseeable" duties to prevent or mitigate future attacks may be poorly bounded, problematic to estimate, and, consequently, difficult to insure fully.[47]

Maritime Security Regulations: A Source of Duty for Potential Tortfeasors

In the wake of the September 11 attacks, both U.S. regulations and international maritime security conventions were strengthened to protect against potential terrorist threats. Related international rules were established in December 2002 under the International Ship and Port Facility Security (ISPS) Code, as an amendment to the International Convention for the Safety of Life at Sea (SOLAS).[48] At around the same time, the United States passed a complementary set of security provisions under the auspices of the Maritime Transportation Security Act of 2002 (MTSA) (46 USCS 70101–70117). Both U.S. and international authorities have now adopted a set of requirements designed

---

[47] To the extent that even very low probability but catastrophic events are deemed legally foreseeable, then defendants could be liable for a poorly defined set of risks that are not merely expensive to insure, but very difficult even to actuarialize based on past experience.

[48] See discussion of SOLAS and ISPS in Carey (2004, pp. 295–296) and in Schoenbaum and Langston (2003, pp. 1334–1345).

to tighten vessel and port security practices against terrorism. Chief among the related provisions of U.S. law is a mandate for Coast Guard–approved vessel security plans (VSPs) and port facility security plans (FSPs). Pursuant to U.S. regulations under MTSA, VSPs and FSPs are required to address security through various measures, including personnel training, drills, communications, and specific plans to protect restricted areas and cargo handling processes. The provisions of MTSA apply to most cargo and passenger ships that either depart from or are bound to U.S. ports (33 CFR 104.105), and MTSA requires that vessels and facilities actually comply with their approved security plans as a condition for their continuing operation (see 46 USCS 71103[c][5]). Apart from MTSA, the United States has also instituted several other programs and requirements designed to improve maritime and supply chain security against terrorist threats, including the Containerized Shipping Initiative (CSI), the Customs-Trade Partnership Against Terrorism (C-TPAT), the Proliferation Security Initiative (PSI), and the Coast Guard's 24-Hour Rule.[49]

For purposes of determining civil liability, MTSA and other U.S. legal requirements for vessel and port security are important because those mandates set standards that could become tied into civil suits following a maritime terrorist attack. For example, when vessel owners or maritime facility operators violate the terms of their own security plans under MTSA then become targets in an attack, the failure to fulfill those security plans will likely become a focus for civil liability. Once again, under the legal doctrine of negligence per se, violation of a statutory safety requirement is generally grounds for presuming fault against a party (e.g., a carrier), at least when that violation results in an injury to someone whom the law was intended to protect.[50] Likewise, under the Pennsylvania Rule, violation of a statutory safety standard may also be grounds for presuming the causation of damages, in connection with an alleged maritime tort. Even though maritime terrorist attacks involve the independent criminal activities of third parties,

---

[49] For a discussion of several of these additional security initiatives, see Willis and Ortiz (2004). See also Bishop (2002, pp. 318–324).

[50] See generally discussion in Keeton and Prosser (1984, pp. 220–233).

where vessels and port facilities have both defined their own security plans and agreed to uphold them under MTSA, violation of those plans would seem to fall squarely within the negligence per se and Pennsylvania Rule doctrines. Exactly how U.S. maritime laws will ultimately structure and resolve civil claims in the wake of a terrorist attack will depend both on the facts of the attack and on applicable maritime and admiralty statutes, described previously. But a key element to recognize is that U.S. laws governing vessel and port security, though silent as to the issue of civil liability, may nevertheless bear directly on the standard of care that is required in operating vessels and port facilities in the United States, and on the liability of parties who breach that standard.

Maritime Terrorism, Supply Chain Disruption, and Contractual Liability

In addition to generating tort claims, some maritime terrorist attacks could plausibly generate significant contractual liability as well. In particular, terrorist attacks on containerized shipping are likely to involve harm to cargo at minimum and, in some scenarios, could be targeted at damaging port facilities or disrupting cargo traffic through U.S. seaports. As demonstrated by the 2002 experience with the labor lockout at the port of Los Angeles, even a short-term closure of a seaport can result in very significant economic disruptions.[51] Shipments of goods and commodities through seaports can often entail a lengthy series of elaborate contractual relationships between the originators of goods, maritime carriers, port facilities, land-based carriers, the immediate recipients of goods, and more distant downstream commercial interests. Any disruption of port operations by a maritime terrorist attack has the potential to interrupt the supply chain, with the result of disrupting all subsequent transactions in goods further down the chain. From an economic perspective, this kind of disruption can result in cascading commercial losses to many private sector firms, with effects

---

[51] See description in Hall (2004).

felt far beyond the direct physical site of a maritime attack (see Chapter Three in regard to the consequences of attacks).[52] From a legal standpoint, a terrorist-induced supply chain disruption raises the possibility that an initial party in the supply chain will be forced into default on its own bilateral contractual obligations, with the result of forcing a series of domino-like defaults in subsequent, downstream contracts. The liability consequences of this kind of cascade turn on a simple question: How will the law deal with broken or unfulfilled contracts, in the context of a maritime terrorist attack?

In principle, the answer to this question turns partly on the terms of specific contracts that are either broken or rendered unfulfillable by an attack and partly on the provisions of the Uniform Commercial Code (UCC), a set of general background terms that applies to most U.S. transactions in goods.[53] Notably, the UCC defines some standard contractual provisions by which a seller of goods can obligate itself to undertake shipment to a purchaser, while the seller retains associated risks and expenses (see UCC 2-319). Failure by a seller to deliver goods under a contract would ordinarily result in default, except where the terms of the contract or the UCC provide an exception. Notably, the UCC includes a provision excusing a seller's nonperformance of delivery based on impracticability, this given the occurrence of a contingency (such as a terrorist attack) "the non-occurrence of which was a basic assumption on which the contract was made" (UCC 2-615[a]). It is likely that this UCC provision will cover at least some instances of contractual nonperformance of the delivery of goods, in the context of

---

[52] Many sectors of the American economy may be particularly vulnerable to this kind of supply chain disruption, because of the widespread adoption of just-in-time inventory practices.

[53] Recall also that maritime contracts for the shipment of goods between U.S. ports or into U.S. ports from overseas will be subject to the Harter Act or to COGSA, which operate to impose duties of reasonable care on vessel owners while immunizing them against liability for cargo losses provided that those duties of care are met. When the Harter Act or COGSA applies, the parties to a shipping contract will be restricted in their ability to contract around the default liability rules imposed by statute.

a supervening terrorist event.[54] More generally, the impact of a terrorist attack on contractual obligations is likely to turn on the interpretation of standard contract provisions, such as force majeure clauses,[55] which arguably could excuse nonperformance in the context of an attack. The most challenging cases of contractual nonperformance are those in which a contract is silent or ambiguous as to the parties' intent regarding a contingency like terrorism. In those cases, courts are compelled to interpret the contract's terms in light of precedent and customary commercial practice, to try to infer what the parties would have agreed to had they contemplated the contingency.

In practice, ambiguities about the contractual implications of terrorism are probably less important now than they were prior to the September 11 attacks. In the wake of those attacks, it is fairly clear that terrorism is a risk that broadly affects many commercial transactions, including maritime cargo contracts and transactions in goods. Whenever two parties to a contract are specifically aware of a risk or contingency as they enter into an agreement, they can always write terms into the agreement explicitly to address that contingency. Presumably this is now the case with regard to many transactions in goods and maritime contracts, given that the risks of terrorism are now universally salient. By implication, contractual liability problems in future maritime terrorist attacks are likely to be somewhat less important than tort problems. They will also likely be trumped by the underlying disruptions to commerce and the supply chain that could likely result from an attack upon, or damage to, a U.S. seaport. Recall again that contractual liability, like tort liability, fundamentally involves a set of rules for shifting costs associated with an injury. Even where explicit

---

[54] See generally discussion in Baker (2004, pp. 14–21). Although formal default rules in contract (as under the UCC) will likely help to reduce future civil claims, the reality of another catastrophic attack will inevitably generate new disputes over the interpretation of contract terms, particularly where the allocation of extremely large losses hangs in the balance.

[55] The expression *force majeure* refers to a contract clause intended to protect the parties in the event that a part of the contract cannot be performed due to causes that are outside the control of the parties and could not be avoided by exercise of reasonable care (Garner and Black, 2000, p. 520).

contract terms eliminate liability associated with an impracticable contract, the underlying economic injuries to the participants may remain overwhelming. Thus, the economic effects of supply chain disruption in some maritime terrorism scenarios are likely to be highly consequential, even though civil liability for broken contract provisions may be expressly limited or nonexistent.

Discussion: Liability, Insurance, and Policy

In the wake of a maritime terrorist attack, injured persons and property owners will have an incentive to seek compensation for their injuries from any available resource. The immediate plaintiffs in civil claims will be the parties directly injured by an attack, and the magnitude of their claims will be determined by the nature and extent of the harm. Civil liability rules offer a mechanism for shifting the costs of injury from one party to another, consistent with legal standards for fault, causation, and negligence in tort and for default in contract. The immediate defendants in civil claims will be parties whose commercial or property interests are touched or targeted in a terrorist attack: parties who arguably could have prevented or mitigated an attack through their own conduct and who arguably owe duties of care to foreseeable victims. The specific legal standards and precedents that will apply to determining liability in particular maritime terrorism scenarios are complex and fact-dependent. Some maritime attacks will focus entirely on vessels on navigable water, where U.S. admiralty jurisdiction and a special set of maritime laws are likely to apply. Other maritime attacks may target facilities on land or may involve land-based negligence by commercial entities in the performance of security functions on shore—facts that are likely to implicate nonmaritime liability rules under applicable state and federal laws. Regardless, core tort claims will likely arise in virtually any maritime terrorist attack. These claims will likely draw on the traditional elements of negligence, with defendants being accused of breaching duties to plaintiffs by failing to take reasonable measures to protect plaintiffs from foreseeable harm.

Negligence liability for the independent acts of third parties turns on the notion of foreseeability. At common law, this notion resulted in only limited tort liability risk, because the criminal acts of third parties were frequently viewed as being unforeseeable. But the attacks of September 11 have changed the meaning of *foreseeability*, by making the risks of terrorism and catastrophic losses in the U.S. impossible to ignore. Exactly how foreseeability will be dealt with in future maritime terrorism cases is difficult to predict. But one plausible interpretation is that virtually all maritime terrorist threats, no matter how unlikely, could be viewed henceforth as foreseeable and might therefore demand corresponding duties of reasonable care on the part of commercial interests and property owners. The problem with this viewpoint is that potential maritime terrorist attacks present a heterogeneous and nebulous set of threats that may be difficult to apprehend in complete detail, and the *legal* foreseeability of any particular attack is only clear in hindsight. In other words, where foreseeable risk encompasses an innumerable set of low-likelihood but highly consequential events, the likely result is expansive civil liability for commercial interests, together with ambiguity about what sorts of protective measures and priorities are actually required under the law.[56] Ideally, civil liability rules are supposed to shift the costs of negligent injuries to the parties responsible for causing them and to incentivize appropriate precautions and insurance against risk. As applied to terrorism, though, evolving liability rules could have a very different effect: namely, to take a broad set of risks to society at large and, paradoxically, to focus related costs onto a limited set of commercial interests in a manner that makes those costs difficult to ensure.[57]

One of the prime implications of civil liability in maritime terrorism involves its effect on commercial insurers and insurance prod-

---

[56] In other words, as negligence doctrine becomes more expansive and less wedded to meaningful standards that define the duty of care, the liability doctrine will begin to look increasingly like strict liability and less like negligence.

[57] This kind of liability effect is also troubling in light of past empirical studies that suggest that self-protective behavior undertaken by firms against terrorist attacks may simply encourage terrorists to substitute more vulnerable targets. See, e.g., Lakdawalla and Zanjani (2004). This is not the end result that civil liability incentives are supposed to achieve.

ucts. By now, the post–September 11 history of U.S. government inter-
vention to backstop both the airlines and private-sector insurance and
reinsurance mechanisms is widely known.[58] In the aftermath of the
September 11 attacks, insurers and reinsurers began to drop coverage
for terrorism from their policies, having recognized a poorly defined
but potentially very large set of terrorism risks.[59] With the government
assumption of related risks under the Terrorism Risk Insurance Act
of 2002 (TRIA), insurers returned to the market for providing terrorism risk coverage and began to reformulate their policies and contracts in order to delimit and value terrorism risks better (see Chalk
et al., 2005). Traditional terms in maritime insurance policies had
involved significant ambiguity over the extent to which terrorist acts
might be covered, under various provisions relating to civil commo-
tions, barratry, piracy, and war risks.[60] Greater clarity has reportedly
emerged following September 11, with clearer exclusions for terrorism
risks written into maritime policies for hull insurance and property
and indemnity (P&I) insurance, and with separate protection against
terrorism risks expressly offered through the mechanism of multiple
levels of war risk insurance coverage (see International Group of P&I
Clubs, 2005). But despite the improved clarity in maritime insurance
contracting (and presumably in other types of insurance contracting as
well), underlying civil liability risks connected with terrorism remain
difficult to estimate for potential commercial defendants, as well as
for the insurers who cover them. Given the uncertainties in this liabil-

---

[58] See generally, e.g., Chalk et al. (2005). Regarding the federal effort to backstop the airlines following September 11, see Lewinsohn (2005). Note that ATSSSA both established
the 9/11 Victims' Compensation Fund and provided support to airlines in the form of a cap
on their liability, plus direct compensatory payments from government of more than $4 bil-
lion. As Lewinsohn (2005) observed, ATSSSA achieved only mixed success in stabilizing a
weakened domestic airline industry.

[59] An interesting anecdotal example of liability risk involves specific insurance contracting provisions relating to the World Trade Center complex and the question of whether the
attacks on the two towers constituted separate "occurrences" for purposes of determining
insurance liability. More than $3 billion of potential liability turns on the interpretation of
occurrences under the relevant insurance contracts. See discussion in Waller and Warrington
(2004).

[60] See generally discussion in Danoff (2003–2004) and Staring (2003).

ity landscape, it should come as little surprise that Congress recently decided to extend TRIA and to continue offering its backstop to insurers (Pub. L. 109-144).

For maritime commercial interests, the challenge posed by civil liability is to take reasonable care against a broad set of legally foreseeable terrorist threats and to obtain insurance sufficient to cover the remote possibility of highly consequential attacks with severe liability. For the justice system and for policymakers, the challenge is to review whether traditional civil liability rules and negligence doctrines make sense as applied to maritime terrorist attacks. Third-party liability is, at least in theory, a device for creating optimal incentives to those private-sector parties who are best positioned to prevent or mitigate attacks. But the incentives only work where terrorism risks are knowable and reasonably well-defined and where legal standards do not result in unlimited civil liability after the fact.[61] September 11 and TRIA demonstrate the likelihood that the federal government may become an insurer of last resort in the event of future catastrophic terrorist events. Where the government actually steps into that role, it suggests a set of risks and costs that are inconsistent with traditional legal notions of foreseeability and that perhaps might be better understood instead as aggregate risks and costs to society. The key question then becomes this: If tort liability as applied to maritime terrorism is effective neither in generating appropriate private-sector incentives nor in capturing terrorism risks in a way that facilitates private-sector insurance mechanisms, does it then become more sensible to remove the compensation of terrorism victims entirely from the traditional mechanisms of civil justice?

The answer to this question is fundamentally one for policymakers to decide (although passage of TRIA and of the Victims' Compensation Fund after September 11 is at least suggestive of standing concerns about the adequacy of conventional compensation mechanisms in the

---

[61] Catastrophic terrorism may violate both of these preconditions. More generally, where (1) damages from terrorism threaten to exceed the assets of firms dramatically, (2) firms compete to shift terrorism risks toward their competitors, and (3) terrorists actively seek to compensate for the precautions taken by firms, civil liability incentives are unlikely to achieve their theoretical objectives.

aftermath of a major attack). With regard to future acts of maritime terrorism, there are several potential targets for more limited, incremental reforms. First, private firms engaged in maritime commerce may be in the best position to evaluate their own unique tort liability risks, based both on their business operations and on applicable laws. In consequence, firms would be well advised to review their own exposure to terrorism liability, as one part of their broader risk-management efforts. Second, U.S. legal standards for tort liability connected with maritime attacks are currently split across multiple statutory and common law authorities at both state and federal levels. This fragmentation makes legal analysis of these sorts of problems more challenging and, over time, it could result in the evolution of inconsistent liability standards in connection with different terrorist attacks. Fragmentation raises the question whether third-party liability presents a sufficiently distinctive problem to justify legislation to simplify and harmonize related rules, against the existing backdrop of various admiralty and nonadmiralty laws that might otherwise apply. Finally, and on a related note, policymakers will eventually be compelled to address the ambiguity of foreseeability of harm as the defining criterion for negligence related to terrorist attacks. The justice system, by its nature, cannot resolve this ambiguity until it arises in future cases. Again, policymakers may want to consider dealing with the issue more proactively, in support of better incentives and more stable insurance mechanisms *ex ante*, and swifter, more certain compensation for victims *ex post*.

CHAPTER FIVE

Risks of Maritime Terrorism Attacks Against Cruise Ships

Every year, millions of people around the world include cruise vacations in their leisure travel plans. As of January 1, 2004, 339 active ocean-going liners were operating around the world with a combined weight of some 10.9 million gross tons. Included in this global fleet were vessels capable of carrying well in excess of 1,000 people—the *Queen Mary 2*, for instance, carries up to 3,900 passengers and crew members—although most ships are of the lower berth category with an average passenger load of 224 (Ebersold, 2004; Cunard, undated).

Despite being a global industry, the cruise business is quite geographically and economically concentrated. Ten companies control more than 60 percent of the market. Approximately 12 million paying customers were projected to have taken a cruise in 2004, 78 percent of whom were from North America, 18 percent from Europe, and 4 percent from Asia and the South Pacific. The bulk of this traffic was concentrated in the Caribbean (46 percent), followed by the Mediterranean (21 percent) and Alaska (8 percent) (Ebersold, 2004). For North America, this translates into more than 9 million passengers contributing approximately $14.7 billion to the U.S. economy (Business Research and Economic Advisors, 2005).

Historically, cruise ships have been targets for terrorism. One notable attack occurred on October 7, 1985, when four men representing the PLF hijacked the *Achille Lauro*. Ultimately, the hijackers killed one passenger, were unsuccessful in achieving their demands for the release of Palestinians held in Israeli prisons, and were convicted in Italian courts.

This chapter provides an overview of the nature and magnitude of risks of terrorist attacks on cruise ships. Of the numerous scenarios that could be imagined, this chapter focuses on the following six to demonstrate the diversity of threats, vulnerabilities, and potential consequences that surround terrorist risks to cruise ships:

- *Hijacking of a cruise ship and its passengers*: Similar to the *Achille Lauro* attack in which a cruise ship is boarded and commandeered while perpetrators hold and potentially injure or kill passengers if demands are not met.
- *Sinking a ship using a boat-borne IED*: Similar to the USS *Cole* and M/V *Limburg* attacks in which a small boat loaded with high explosives is rammed into a ship and detonated. As noted above, in 2005 an al Qaeda–linked militant, Lu'ai Sakra, was implicated in a strike of this sort against Israeli cruise ships carrying tourists to Turkey.
- *Sinking a ship with a submersible parasitic device*: Though never detected or attempted against a cruise ship, in this scenario, divers would place a high-explosive device on the hull of a ship in an effort to sink the vessel.
- *Bombing on board a ship*: A suicide bomber boards a ship and detonates a bomb in an effort to kill or injure passengers.
- *Standoff attack on ship using heavy artillery*: Similar to the pirate attack on the *Seabourn Spirit*[1] in 2005, perpetrators attack a ship from land or boat using grenade launchers, mortars, or shoulder-fired missiles in an effort to kill or injure passengers.
- *Biological attack on a ship's food or water supply*: With anticipated consequences similar to the Norwalk virus outbreak on the *Mariner of the Seas* ("Virus Strikes Cruise Ship," 2005), in this scenario, terrorists contaminate a ship's food or water supply with a biological weapon.

---

[1]   The liner, which was en route from Egypt to Mombasa, Kenya, with 302 passengers and crew members, was attacked with machine-gun fire and RPGs after it strayed too close to the Somali shore. Although no one was seriously injured in the assault, the incident caught the headlines of major newspapers around the world, many of whom focused on the fact that the ship was carrying mostly Western tourists. See "Cruise Ship Repels Somali Pirates" (2005).

Attractiveness of Cruise Ships as Targets of Terrorism

There are several facets of the luxury-oriented, yet highly popular cruise liner industry that would appear to have particular relevance for future terrorist attack contingencies. Most fundamentally, these vessels constitute an attractive target that directly resonates with the underlying ideological and operational rationale of al Qaeda and the wider international jihadist movement. Not only do cruise ships cater to large numbers of people who are confined to a single geographic space—which makes them ideal venues for carrying out assaults intended to maximize civilian casualties (a hallmark of jihadist terrorism in the post–September 11 era)—they are also highly iconic in nature, reflecting the type of explicit Western materialism, affluence, and discretionary spending to which bin Laden–inspired extremists are opposed.[2] Moreover, the fact that an overwhelming majority of passengers on cruise lines are of Judeo-Christian background means that indiscriminate attacks can be carried out with little or no risk of negatively affecting wider Muslim interests (anonymous former defense intelligence official, 2005). This is not necessarily the case with land-based incidents, as bombings of Western embassies in Kenya and Tanzania (1998), tourist resorts in Bali (2002), and hotels in Jakarta and Amman (2003 and 2005, respectively) clearly demonstrated.[3]

On a more general level, a decisive strike against a major ocean-going carrier would almost certainly result in a global CNN effect. Indeed, as the November 2005 attack against the *Seabourn Spirit* off the coast of Somalia demonstrates, even comparatively small-scale events have the potential to elicit considerable international media attention and interest. Generating this type of publicity is critical to the dynamics of any terrorist entity, not least because it can be readily exploited to

---

[2]   A dossier captured with Nashiri in 2003 specifically listed cruise liners sailing from Western ports among al Qaeda's targets of opportunity, highlighting their "attractiveness" in terms of mass casualty attacks. See Köknar (2005) and English, Gallagher, and Sommerfeld (2003).

[3]   All of these attacks resulted in inordinately high casualty rates for local Muslims, which, at least in the case of the embassy bombings, far outweighed Western fatalities and injuries.

demonstrate operational vibrancy, which is vital for attracting recruits and boosting the morale of existing cadres.

Vulnerability of Cruise Ships to Terrorist Attacks

Besides being an attractive target, there are also vulnerabilities pertinent to the cruise industry that terrorists could potentially exploit. Although more rigorous since September 11, 2001, security checks remain far less stringent than those employed for commercial aviation. According to UK officials, while prominent British companies like Cunard require all boarding passengers to pass through a metal detector and x-ray all carry-on luggage, only about 2 percent of those embarking ships are physically inspected. Moreover, under normal circumstances bags are not scanned before they are transferred to cabins. In addition, while virtually all major operators thoroughly vet their own crew and maintenance staff, many of the service employees who have access to ships at overseas docks may not have undergone any form of comprehensive background checking. These personnel, who are often highly receptive to bribes and other forms of subversion (given the low wages they are routinely paid), offer terrorists a ready conduit through which to smuggle and stash weapons or explosives for subsequent attacks (anonymous UK customs and excise officials, 2005).

Besides these problems, there are certain operational traits that could conceivably open up cruise ships to possible terrorist risks. Vessels frequently anchor off shore for extended periods of time (sometimes up to 24 hours) to allow those on board an opportunity to sight-see and take day trips. It is during these prolonged stops that a liner would be most exposed to a collision assault—either from a fast approach and explosive-laden suicide craft or a more sizable boat (2,000+ tonnage) that is deliberately smashed into its side (anonymous Control Risks Group [Netherlands] personnel and Department of Homeland Security Liaison attache, 2005). The traditional practice of passengers congregating on upper decks and waving to onlookers, friends, and relatives at a departing port could be just as problematic in terms of inviting attacks, particularly land-based strikes involving flat trajectory weapons such as rocket-propelled grenades (RPGs), missiles, shoulder-launched missiles, and sniper rifles (anonymous former defense intelligence official, 2005).

Finally, virtually all luxury liners sail according to precise schedules and preplanned itineraries that are readily available through the Internet, advertising brochures, or travel agents. This information constitutes a highly valuable source of intelligence for terrorists, allowing a perpetrating group to pick the time and place for easiest covert expedition of transfer of explosives and operatives to a targeted vessel or when a ship will be most susceptible to a mid-sea assault. Though this does not distinguish cruise ships from other modes of public transportation, it does provide information that contributes to their vulnerability to attack. Such advanced knowledge, if adroitly exploited, would help to offset greatly the uncertainty that is normally associated with attack planning and logistics (anonymous Control Risks Group [UK] personnel and Department of Homeland Security Liaison attache, 2005).

While these vulnerabilities make cruise ships potentially susceptible to many types of terrorist attack, most experts agree that sinking a cruise liner would be extremely difficult. These vessels are built with safety as a foremost priority. Hulls are double-lined and, in most cases, interiors are compartmentalized with largely if not fully watertight systems in place.[4] Attempting to overcome these safeguards through an on-board explosion would require several highly powerful bombs as well as a sophisticated understanding of the structural integrity of the target in question, particularly in terms of being able to discern quickly and accurately locations where explosions could be expected to cause the most damage (anonymous International Maritime Bureau personnel, 2005).

An external small-boat ramming attack has a far greater prospect of causing extensive damage. However, even here, the possibility of a critical breach is questionable. In the United States, the security mea-

---

4 It would be impossible to construct a cruise liner that has a fully compartmentalized, watertight system in place, as the recreational and luxury-oriented nature of these vessels necessarily requires an on-board configuration that is open and accessible (within the constraints of allowable safety limits).

sures that are put in place around cruise ships as they enter and dock in port provide an outer layer of defense against this type of attack. Moreover, the suicide strikes on the USS *Cole* and M/V *Limburg* highlight the general difficulty of critically damaging a large ocean-going vessel if the site of impact does not correlate with weak points in the craft's "skeleton" design.

Another terrorist option for sinking a cruise liner is through an underwater attack, specifically by attaching mines or other "parasitic devices" to a berthed ship's hull.[5] Although possible, this type of combat diving requires considerable training and skill both requiring swimming undetected and avoiding the high volume of traffic that typically traverses major maritime terminals.[6] Moreover, in the case of a shallow-water port such as Rotterdam, the net effect of a submersible strike would merely be to cause the stricken vessel to settle on the bottom of the seabed, not to sink it (anonymous Control Risks Group [Netherlands] personnel and independent maritime expert, 2005).

There are several other terrorist scenarios, however, that, while somewhat less dramatic in manifestation, could still elicit considerable fear, damage, or publicity. In each of these cases, the relative freedom of movement throughout a ship and comparatively low level of screening feasible for passengers and crew leave cruise ships potentially vulnerable to attack. For instance, a group could bomb venues where passengers routinely congregate for relaxation and recreation on board, including restaurants, casinos, and cinemas. Plastic or C4 explosive would be well suited for this type of attack, as it is both hard to detect and highly malleable in nature (which means it can be broken down

---

[5] It would be highly difficult to carry out an attack of this sort against a moving ship, given the extremely strong currents and undertow that its engines would necessarily generate. The U.S. government issued a warning in spring 2002 specifically highlighting the threat posed to cruise liners by "swimmers" attaching incendiary devices to ship hulls. See Sinai (2004, p. 65) and Newman (2003).

[6] Anonymous Control Risks Group (Netherlands) personnel (2005). One group that is acknowledged to have mastered combat scuba techniques is the LTTE. Indeed, the Tigers are known to have developed their own two-person mini submarine specifically for the purpose of covertly debussing divers inside Sri Lankan harbors (anonymous Sri Lankan intelligence officials and Western diplomat, 2005). For further details, see Davis (2000).

and repackaged in everyday items unlikely to raise suspicions). A series of random killings or hostage-takings could also be staged, using either basic weapons that are accessible on board (for example, knives stolen from kitchen galleys) or more lethal assault rifles and pistols that had already been predeployed by co-opted members of the crew. Similarly, an organization could carry out localized acts of arson in areas where fire doors are absent or where sprinkle systems and alarms had first been disabled. Finally, various biological assaults might be possible, ranging from high-tech releases of airborne viruses through a ship's ventilation system, to more rudimentary (and, therefore, arguably more probable) disseminations of foodborne contaminants such as salmonella, E. coli, botulinum toxin, and mercury.[7]

Potential Consequences of Terrorist Attacks on Cruise Ships

The consequences of terrorist strikes on cruise liners are relatively open-ended and depend on the dimensions of the ship attacked; extent of damage caused to the vessel; and how the government, private, and public sectors respond to the event. However, it is possible to bound the potential ramifications of various scenarios by considering the size of passenger liners, the size of the cruise ship industry, and economic effects of previous terrorism events that have actually taken place. An assessment of these consequences is provided in Table 5.1.

---

[7] Anonymous UK customs and excise officials, former defense intelligence official, and Control Risks Group (UK) personnel (2005). See also Sinai (2004, p. 65) and Watkins (2002).

Table 5.1
Potential Consequences of Terrorist Attack Scenarios Involving Cruise Ships

Maritime Terrorism Scenario	Potential Human Consequences	Potential Economic Consequences	Potential Intangible Consequences
Hijack ship at sea	Tens to hundreds of fatalities and injuries	Hundreds of millions of dollars in life and injury compensation Hundreds of millions of dollars in increased security Billions of dollars from changes in individual purchasing patterns, such as decreased cruise travel *Cost of response*[a] *Increased insurance rates*[a]	*Loss of human capital*[a]
Ram ship in port with IED	Hundreds to thousands of fatalities and injuries	Same as hijack of a ship, plus hundreds of millions of dollars from repair or loss of ship[b]	
Suicide dive bomber or limpet mine attack	Hundreds to thousands of fatalities and injuries	Same as hijack of a ship, plus hundreds of millions of dollars from repair or loss of ship[b]	
Suicide bombing on ship at port or sea	Tens to hundreds of fatalities and injuries	Same as hijack of a ship	
Standoff mortar or grenade launcher attack	Tens to hundreds of fatalities and injuries	Same as hijack of a ship	
Biological attack on ship food or water	Tens of fatalities and hundreds to thousands of injuries	Same as hijack of a ship	

[a] Bounding cost estimates have not been identified for items in italics.

[b] "Cruise Ship Listing" (undated).

Human Consequences

As mentioned above, the largest cruise ships can carry over 3,000 passengers and 1,000 crew members. Thus, in the most extreme cases, it is theoretically possible that a terrorist attack could claim the lives of several thousand people in a single strike. Even in cases short of a cataclysmic sinking, potential fatalities from a major on-board explosion would probably still number in the dozens, if not the hundreds.

Looking at the 652 suicide bombings in the RAND terrorism database, the median number of deaths and injuries per suicide attack is 5 and 12, respectively. For maritime incidents, the corresponding figures are 1 and 5. Thus, based on empirical evidence from historical bombing attacks, potential consequences can be expected to result in tens to, at most, hundreds of fatalities and injuries. This magnitude of human consequences would appear comparable for standoff artillery attacks or even ship hijackings that included fatalities, assuming munitions of a comparative size were used.

Historical evidence of contagious disease outbreaks on land and at sea provides benchmarks for the human consequences of biological attacks on cruise ships. Though a sophisticated strike on a cruise ship using weaponized anthrax or engineered viruses could theoretically kill thousands of people, obtaining such materials and successfully infecting a sufficient number of passengers and crew to achieve these results would be difficult. Successfully carrying out an attack using these pathogens requires resources and capability to obtain and handle the microbe as well as skill to administer an infective dose successfully. In contrast, attacks that have consequences similar to food- and waterborne illnesses require less sophistication and thus may be more likely. Toxins such as botulinum and bacteria such as E. coli and salmonella can be easily produced and handled and are difficult to detect by taste, smell, or color in food or water that has been contaminated. Scenarios involving these agents to could kill tens of people and require treatment of hundreds to thousands of other victims are easily envisioned.

Economic Consequences

Scenarios that present the risk of significant damage to, or loss of, the ship itself could produce direct damages on the order of hundreds of millions of dollars. According to CruiseCrew.com, the largest new cruise ships cost more than $500 million to build ("Cruise Ship Listing," undated). Many of the other potential economic consequences of terrorist attacks on cruise ships are independent of the attack scenario. Rather, they are the product of terrorists deciding to target the cruise industry once, along with the anticipation that additional events may occur in the future. These consequences include compensation for injuries and loss of life, increased security costs associated with future passenger line operations, changes in individual consumption patterns that reduce demand for cruises, costs of the immediate response, and various other capital outlays such as increases in insurance rates.

Compensation for Injuries and Loss of Life

Empirical evidence from previous terrorist attacks provides a benchmark for considering the compensation payments that might follow an attack on a cruise ship. According to "Insurance Claims to Exceed $110m" (2004) and Knight and Pretty (1997), the amounts insured for in the *Estonia* and *Herald of Free Enterprise* ferry disasters are quantified as $70 million and $110 million, respectively. Extrapolating from these figures and accounting for the fact that cruise ships carry significantly more passengers than ferries do, the life and injury compensation expected for scenarios involving catastrophic attacks on cruise liners could be on the order of hundreds of millions of dollars.

Of course, private-sector costs associated with compensating for injuries and loss of life may be strongly affected by the liability rules and the threshold determination on whether operators themselves can be held legally accountable in the context of the facts of a given attack. Depending on future liability rulings, the result could be to open commercial defendants to the possibility of enormous payouts in connection with attacks or to foreclose tort recoveries and allow those costs to remain with the victims. Either way, liability rules do not change the underlying valuation of loss of life in connection with an attack.

Increased Security Costs

An obvious but highly important component of counterterrorism efforts resides in enhanced security measures provided by the government and private companies. Associated costs that might arise in the aftermath of an attack could include one-time capital expenditures as firms build new infrastructure to harden buildings and facilities against attacks. They may also incorporate expenses arising from changes in operational and business processes to account for greater surveillance, increased inspections, or more persistent due diligence before contractual relationships are initiated.

On the government end, these expenditures can be extremely high and will affect the allocation of government spending long after heightened security measures are relaxed (if this ever happens). On the private end, such costs are typically passed on to the consumer in terms of higher prices for services, decreasing demand.

Coughlin, Cohen, and Khan (2002) estimated the costs of security for the airline industry post–September 11 to be roughly $9 billion annually. Certainly, increased security after an attack would be much lower for the cruise industry largely because it receives significantly fewer passengers per year and the United States has many fewer cruise destinations than it has airports. That said, comparing the approximately 12 million cruise passengers each year to the 685 million airline passengers per year, one would still expect security in the cruise industry to be on the order of hundreds of millions of dollars.

Some of the increased costs in private security measures following an attack may plausibly be driven by liability proceedings against commercial defendants. Tort suits against cruise lines (and other associated commercial interests) will be based on the argument that legal duties and standards of care have been breached. At present, those standards of care are uncertain in application and unclear in reach. But following an attack, judgments against commercial defendants may clarify the nature of the duties owed and of the security standards that defendants are required to meet under the law. Perhaps more importantly, large liability judgments against those defendants could create very strong private-sector incentives in guarding against future attacks: incentives that would tend to lead private firms to invest more heavily in preventive security measures.

Declines in Demand for Cruise Vacations

Various studies of the impact of terrorist attacks on tourism suggest that assaults on cruise liners could result in decreased demand for cruise vacations. Frey, Luechinger, and Stutzer (2004), citing Enders, Sandler, and Parise (1991), for instance, estimate that in 1988, 1.5 times as many tourists would have visited Spain, were it not for the 18 terrorist incidents that occurred in the country that year. What this shows is that tourists' preferences to visit a country can be highly elastic with regard to the number of terrorist incidents that occur in it. Thus, it would stand to reason that any terrorist attack would have severe repercussions on a country's tourism base (particularly the two sectors that stand to benefit the most from this industry—travel and lodging).

Terrorism may also affect consumers' decisions about types of vacation travel, not just locations. Ito and Lee (2005) concluded that the September 11 attacks and the attendant security measures put in place after the strikes accounted for approximately 94 percent of the subsequent decline in airline revenue.

It is conceivable that attacks on cruise ships could have a long-term impact of billions of dollars per year. As mentioned previously, the industry reportedly accounts for just over $14.7 billion in economic activity around major American tourist ports including some 315,000 full- and part-time jobs.[8] States that would be most affected by a decrease in the attractiveness of tourism by sea would be Florida, California, and New York which, respectively, spent $5 billion, $1.5 billion, and $1.4 billion in 2004 on cruise ship products (Business Research and Economic Advisors, 2005).

That said, these damages, though significant, are modest when compared to the respective regional economies. According to Bureau of Economic Analysis statistics on gross state product (GSP), this works out to approximately 1 percent of GSP for Florida, 0.1 percent for California, and approximately 0.15 percent for New York. Furthermore, leisure travel is readily substitutable. Individuals who choose not to take cruises will still take vacations and may well take alternative (land-based) holidays in the regions or states that lost business to a drop in demand for cruises.

Other Economic Consequences
Additional economic consequences may result from costs of response and potentially higher insurance rates following terrorist events. The

---

[8]   Figures derived from International Council of Cruise Lines (undated).

former expenditures would include emergency response, medical and public health services, and decontamination as required. Changes in insurance rates would depend on the magnitude of damages and uptake rates of insurance prior to and following the terrorist events.

We have not yet identified reasonable estimates for bounding these sources of economic consequences and, as a result, cannot speculate on whether the costs would be significant.

Intangible Consequences

The principal intangible consequence of maritime terrorist attacks would be the loss of human capital to firms and society at large that result from these incidents. Though this is difficult to quantify in economic terms, the scale of human consequences discussed above does allow for some bounding of these potential impacts. As tragic as the loss of human life would be from these events, assaults that affect a few thousand passengers on a cruise ship would not have a significant effect on the balance of skills and capabilities in the general U.S. workforce. Nevertheless, consequences could be devastating to particular firms if fatalities and injuries included a large proportion of the companies' employee base either as crew or passengers.

Risks of Terrorist Attacks on Cruise Ships

The risk of terrorist attacks on cruise ships can be gleaned from discussions of threat, vulnerability, and consequences in the preceding questions. Using the qualitative risk assessment methodology outlined in the appendix, it is possible to translate these discussions into assessments of terrorism risk.

Assessment of terrorist intent and capability and of cruise ship vulnerability to various types of attacks determines the relative threat of different terrorist cruise line scenarios. As discussed previously, these vessels are attractive for terrorism since there is potential to kill large numbers of people and cause billions of dollars in economic damages, as well as to elicit considerable media attention by attacking a highly visible and symbolic target. At the same time, some attack scenarios are more easily completed than others. An on-board bombing would require only basic skills typical of volunteers to construct a simple improvised explosive and carry it on board. On the other extreme, parasitic bombs would necessitate specialized military skills of underwater maritime combat techniques. Capabilities required for other attack types would fall between these two extremes. Use of standoff artillery would require terrorists to accurately fire mortars or similar weapons, unless they were able to acquire the more sophisticated (and less available) modern self-aiming weapon systems. Similar capability would be required to board and hijack a ship's crew and passengers. Finally, ramming a ship with an IED or contaminating food and water would require basic military and technical training to be able to construct a more sophisticated IED and develop and handle the contaminant. As seen in Figure 5.1, this results in a matrix of cruise ship attack scenarios that are relatively high in terms of intent, spanning a broad range of capabilities.

The actual likelihood of attack depends on both the threat terrorists pose and the chosen targets' vulnerability. As shown in Figure 5.1, threats to cruise ships range from high (on-board bombs, IED attacks, and food or water contamination) to the comparatively low (terrorists piloting a hijacked ship) based on assessments of terrorist capabilities and intentions.[9]

All scenarios score relatively high in terms of terrorists' intentions. However, the vulnerability of liners to attacks varies considerably between scenarios. For example, the design of cruise ships—which are explicitly intended to prevent a vessel from sinking in the event of an accidental hull breach—greatly reduces their exposure to decisive IED and parasitic bomb strikes. Security measures in place around cruise ships while in dock further reduce these vulnerabilities (although, admittedly, procedures employed at U.S. ports may be more heavily enforced than is the case overseas). However, the mere fact that cruise ships accommodate movement of thousands of people on, off, and throughout the vessel creates inherent vulnerabilities to on-board

---

[9]   The assessment of threat is based on the normalized, multiplicative combination of intent and capability assessments, as discussed in the appendix.

Figure 5.1
Assessment of the Capability Required in Scenarios Involving Terrorist Attacks on Cruise Ships and Extent to Which the Scenario Aligns with Terrorist Groups' Intentions

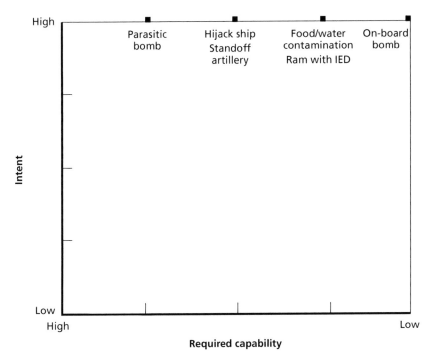

bombings, hijackings, and food or water contamination.[10] As Figure 5.2 shows, the most likely attacks on cruise ships (taking into account both threat and vulnerability) would manifest as either on-board bombings or standoff attacks, and the least likely would be those involving parasitic devices designed to achieve a critical hull breach.

Finally, to determine the relative risk posed by various terrorist attacks on cruise ships, one needs to consider both the likelihood of the assault in question and the potential consequences that might arise

_____

[10] These vulnerabilities are reduced in cases where access to targeted areas can be controlled, such as water distribution systems, food preparation and storage areas, or ship navigation and control rooms.

Figure 5.2
Assessment of the Threat of Terrorist Attacks on Cruise Ships and the
Vulnerability of Cruise Ships to These Attack Scenarios

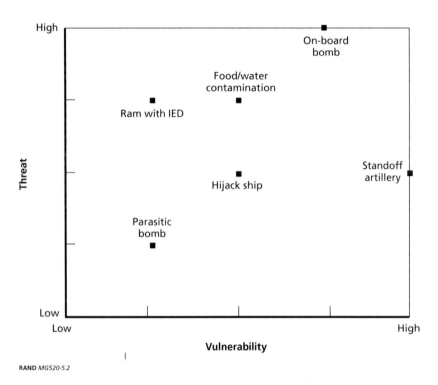

from it. Among scenarios involving maritime terrorism, the most likely are those involving on-board bombing, food or water contamination, and standoff artillery. These scenarios correspond well to perceived intentions and capabilities of terrorist groups and some involve targets that are vulnerable to attack. The least likely of cruise ship scenarios we considered is the use of a parasitic bomb.[11]

The magnitude of consequences of these scenarios seems, at first cut, to be similar across the range of scenarios assessed in this case study. One of the primary economic effects arising from terrorist attacks on cruise liners would be reduced demand for these types of vacations.

------

[11] The assessment of likelihood is based on the normalized, multiplicative combination of threat and vulnerability assessments, as discussed in the appendix.

Though it is unlikely that the ramifications would be catastrophic from a national perspective, they could easily account for the loss of billions of dollars both to the cruise industry and to specific regional economies. These fiscal damages are likely to be significantly larger than any others resulting from life and injury compensation, resources directed to increased security, or costs from damage to or loss of a cruise ship.

The potential human consequences are similarly consistent across scenarios and generally fall into two categories: (1) attacks involving small explosives, hijacking, or food or water contamination, which can be expected to affect tens to hundreds of people; and (2) assaults employing larger munitions, which could potentially kill hundreds to thousands of people, depending on the location of the vessel when it is struck and the extent of damage that befalls the targeted ship.

Figures 5.3 and 5.4 summarize the various themes covered in this chapter. They show that the most realistic attack contingencies pertaining to cruise ships are those that are liable to result in moderate human and economic consequences. In this regard, ramming a vessel with an IED probably represents the greatest relative risk. For human consequences alone, the greatest relative risk is likely to arise from food and water contamination, while from a purely economic perspective, a suicide bombing would seem to carry the most relevance.

Figure 5.3
Assessment of the Relative Likelihood of Terrorist Attacks on Cruise Ships and Potential Economic Consequences of These Attack Scenarios

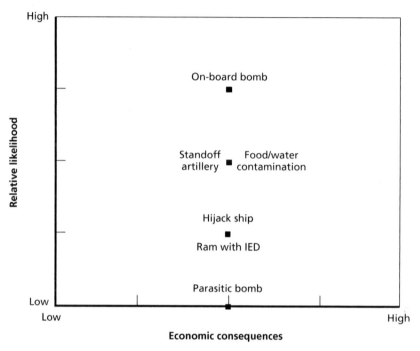

Figure 5.4
Assessment of the Relative Likelihood of Terrorist Attacks on Cruise Ships and Potential Human Consequences of These Attack Scenarios

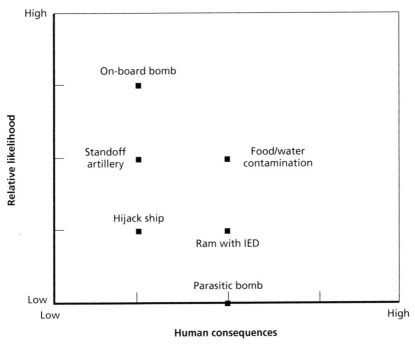

RAND *MG520-5.4*

CHAPTER SIX

Risks of Maritime Terrorism Attacks Against Passenger Ferries

Passenger ferries provide a cheap, highly accessible, and ubiquitous mode of transport on which many people have come to rely as a principal means of national and international movement. Journey times can be as long as 24 hours or as short as 10 minutes, with routes embracing everything from major sea sailings to interisland transits and harbor or river crossings.

Many of the larger vessels currently in operation are able to accommodate a customer base numbering in the thousands. Besides civilians, ferries frequently cater for a wide array of vehicles. Colloquially known as *ro-ros* (roll on, roll off), these craft are designed with expansive open decks immediately above their hulls that allow for the rapid loading and debussing of cars, tourist coaches, buses, minivans, and freight trucks.

As is exemplified by the Port of Dover—the principal maritime gateway to the English Channel and Europe—in Table 6.1, the total volume of traffic passing through a particular hub can quickly add up.

In the United States, more than 66 million passengers travel by ferry each year. Services are provided in approximately 30 urban areas, with the largest networks operating in the Seattle/Tacoma, New York/New Jersey, New Orleans, Boston, and San Francisco Bay areas. Most of these systems service short distances, though in some routes may cover several miles (American Public Transportation Association, 2006, p. 61).

Table 6.1
Ferry Traffic Passing Through the Port of Dover in June 2005

Form of Traffic	Number Moved
Passengers	1,300,000
Cars	259,000
Freight vehicles	180,000
Coaches	12,000

SOURCE: Anonymous UK customs and excise officials (2005).

This chapter provides an overview of the nature and magnitude of the terrorist risk to passenger ferries. Of the numerous attack scenarios that could be imagined, this chapter focuses on the following four to demonstrate the diversity of threats, vulnerabilities, and potential consequences that surround risks of terrorist attack on passenger ferries:

- *Sinking a ship using a boat-borne IED*: Similar to the USS *Cole* and M/V *Limburg* attacks where a small boat loaded with high explosives is rammed into the ship and detonated.
- *Sinking a ship with a submersible parasitic device*: Though never detected or attempted, in this scenario, divers would place a high-explosive device on the hull of a ship in an effort to sink the vessel.
- *Suicide bombing on board a ship*: A suicide bomber boards a ship and detonates in an effort to kill or injure passengers.
- *Standoff attack on ship using artillery*: Similar to the pirate attack on the *Seabourn Spirit*,[1] perpetrators attack the ship from land or boat using grenade launchers, mortars, or shoulder-fired missiles in an effort to kill or injure passengers.

---

[1] The liner, which was en route from Egypt to Mombasa, Kenya, with 302 passengers and crew, was attacked with machine-gun fire and RPGs after it strayed too close to the Somali shore. Although no one was seriously injured in the assault, the incident caught the headlines of major newspapers around the world, many of which focused on the fact that the ship was carrying mostly Western tourists. See "Cruise Ship Repels Somali Pirates" (2005).

Attractiveness of Ferries as Targets of Terrorism

Ferries are certainly not as iconic or prestige a target as are cruise ships, nor do they constitute the same type of high economic value associated with container shipping. That said, several traits inherent to passenger ferries make them especially attractive to terrorist aggression. Principally, attacks on ferries are easy to execute, have the potential to kill many people, are likely to capture significant media attention and can be exploited to visibly demonstrate a terrorist group's salience and vibrancy.

Perhaps the best example of the positive cost-benefit ratio associated with terrorist ferry attacks[2] was the explosion that partially sunk *SuperFerry 14* in the Philippines on February 27, 2004. Although costing only between $300 and $400 and involving less than 5 kilograms of TNT, the bombing killed 116, wounded over 300, garnered considerable coverage in the press, and thrust the hitherto moribund ASG back into the limelight of international terrorist attention.[3]

Thus, it would seem reasonable to speculate that the motivation for terrorists' targeting ferries in the United States would be principally based on the perceived vulnerability and potential consequences of these scenarios.

Vulnerabilities of Ferries to Terrorist Attack

Several factors contribute to passenger ferries' perceived vulnerability to terrorist attack. First, extant security measures at passenger terminals vary greatly. Even in developed littoral states such as the Netherlands, Canada, the United Kingdom, and the United States, they are not nearly as extensive as those employed for cruise liners, much less

---

[2] It should be noted that although commonly accepted as an act of terrorism, there have been some suggestions that the *SuperFerry 14* was targeted because its owners had not complied with ASG demands for protection money. Claims to this effect have been made by officials with the ATTF as well as by Philippine Transport Security Leandro Mendoza. See Republic of the Philippines (2004).

[3] Anonymous Anti-Terrorism Task Force officials (2005). See also Elegant (2004).

for commercial aviation. This is an inevitable fallout from the need to move high volumes of embarking traffic in as efficient a manner as possible, which necessarily precludes the option of carrying out concerted checks on baggage, cars, trucks, and people.[4] Under such circumstances, it would be relatively easy for terrorists to smuggle weapons onto a ferry for an on-board attack, including driving an explosive-rigged vehicle set to detonate when the vessel is fully laden.

Indeed, the institution of even minimal precautionary measures can have the effect of generating huge delays and backlogs. Dover provides a case in point. In the immediate aftermath of the July 2005 London underground bombings, all motorists bound for Calais were subjected to a slightly more rigorous regime of predeparture scrutiny and examination. Although individual inspections and questions generally took no more than a few minutes per vehicle, combined they served to create queues that extended over four miles (anonymous UK customs and excise officials, 2005).

Second, vetting of those working on-board ferries is ad hoc and partial, reflecting the seasonal and highly transient nature of these personnel. Background checks, to the extent that they occur, are generally aimed at verifying past employers and rarely embrace wider criminal investigations. Throughout much of Asia and Africa, it is unlikely that any consistent form of examination takes place, largely because owners and operators lack the means (and frequently the willingness) to do so. Maritime experts generally concur that the absence of effective staff and crew scrutiny represents a significant point of vulnerability for commercial ferry companies, providing extremists with an ideal opening to place insiders covertly on board targeted vessels for strike or logistical purposes.

---

[4] In Britain, for instance, cars and coaches are inspected on a random, selective basis. Freight vehicles are rarely, if ever checked (especially those bearing the Trans International Routier (TIR) insignia—see Chapter Seven). As one former defense intelligence official opined: "Ferries are their own worst enemies: [the industry is] designed to transport a high volume of people as conveniently, cheaply, and quickly as possible. Most operators simply do not have the infrastructure—or willingness—to carry out a comprehensive regimen of security checks" (anonymous former defense intelligence official, 2005).

Several commentators argue that dangers are further exacerbated—at least in the context of the post–September 11 international extremist-Islamist threat—by the overwhelming number of North Africans, Arabs, Muslim Filipinos, and Indonesians whom owner-operators typically hire to fill service positions on their ships. This employment bias is viewed as potentially worrisome in that it affords al Qaeda cohorts and affiliates with a perfect cover that allows them to take advantage of one of the key principles emphasized in jihadist field and training manuals—to "hide in plain sight" whenever possible (anonymous Department of Homeland Security Liaison attache and former defense intelligence official, 2005).

Third, and in common with cruise liners, ferries sail along pre-defined routes according to set departure and arrival times.[5] By definition, these schedules have to be made widely available to the paying public and, as a result, are easily accessed through a broad array of mediums and conduits, ranging from travel guides and port terminals to the Internet. Itineraries are, in short, both fixed and highly transparent, availing terrorists with a reasonably accurate cartographic picture that can be used to gauge the point at which vessels are most susceptible to attack and interception. The ASG in the southern Philippines provides a good example of an organization that has conspicuously planned many of its maritime assaults around information of this sort (anonymous Anti-Terrorism Task Force officials and former defense intelligence official, 2005).

Finally, certain features in the specific construction of ferries serve to weaken their wider structural integrity and safety. As noted above, ro-ros are deliberately built with large open car decks to avail the efficient embarkation and disembarkation of vehicles. Crucially, this particular design format makes these vessels acutely sensitive to subtle shifts in their center of gravity, largely because they lack stabilizing bulkheads on their lower sections. Undue movements of improperly secured auto-

---

5   Also similar to cruise liners, the fixed schedule of ferries does not significantly differentiate ferries from other modes of public transportation though does contribute to their vulnerability of attack.

mobiles or sudden accumulations of even small amounts of water[6] are especially likely to trigger such effects and could, depending on the severity of the situation at hand, cause a ship to list or to capsize fully.[7] As one high-ranking official with the International Maritime Bureau (IMB) in London put it: "One [event] and that's it; these boats have no damage limitation at all" (anonymous International Maritime Bureau personnel, 2005).

Fast cats, a rapid passenger-only ferry that is used extensively in many parts of the world for short interisland crossings and river trips, suffer from different but potentially equally serious vulnerabilities. To facilitate speed, these craft have a minimal superstructure that is typically developed from lightweight metal alloys such as aluminum. Hulls, consequently, tend to be thinner than steel hulls, which makes them extremely susceptible to critical breach from either external or internal sources. Moreover, because outer shells are based on a material (aluminum) that has a relatively low ignition temperature, the possibility of a primary attack spawning a large-scale secondary fire (together with all the smoke and heat that this would entail) is high (anonymous International Maritime Bureau personnel and former defense intelligence official, 2005).

Of all the types of shipping covered in this chapter, ferries are probably the most vulnerable to terrorist aggression, given the structural nature of the vessels and the highly open environment in which they operate.

---

[6] According to one U.S.-based maritime security analyst, as little as a foot of water accumulated in a single location could upset a ship's center of gravity (anonymous Maritime Intelligence Group analyst, 2005).

[7] It should be noted that certain countries have moved to address this specific structural vulnerability. In the United Kingdom, for instance, ferries are now constructed with drains in their car decks to prevent the free-surface effect. Many also have additional buoyancy devices, such as air-filled tanks strapped to either side of the vessel (anonymous UK customs and excise officials, 2005).

Potential Consequences of Terrorist Attacks on Ferries

Three factors determine the potential consequences of terrorist strikes on passenger ferries: the magnitude of the attack, how extensive damage to the ship is, and how people change their behavior in the months following the attack.

For the attacks considered, only human consequences are likely to vary significantly between scenarios. All of the postulated scenarios have the potential for causing significant damage to the vessel and being large enough to result in considerable indirect economic consequences. As with cruise liners, a mass casualty event is likely to have acute political ramifications and may well elicit strong domestic pressure for the initiation of mitigation measures that extend far beyond the maritime realm.

The overall consequences are bounded by the size of ferry boats and criticality of passenger ferries for regional transportation in different areas. Table 6.2 provides an overview of assessment of the potential consequences for attack scenarios presented in this chapter and discussed below.

Human Consequences

The most significant determinant of fatalities and injuries resulting from attacks on passenger ferries is the extent of damage to the vessel. The largest ferries operating today hold 1,500 passengers and a very minimal crew. Scenarios involving significant damage could easily result in several hundred fatalities. The greater the damage, the more likely it will be that the vessel will sink and the higher the death toll would be.

The Abu Sayyaf ferry bombing that caused 116 deaths (Manalo, 2004) is a good example of the minimal capabilities terrorist groups need to possess in order to execute attacks with damaging and far-reaching effects. Other good indicators of the scale of the potential loss of life can be derived from accidents such as the 1994 sinking of the *Estonia* in the Baltic Sea, which resulted in 852 deaths, and the 1987

Table 6.2
Potential Consequences of Terrorist Attack Scenarios Involving Ferry Boats

Maritime Terrorism Scenario	Potential Human Consequences	Potential Economic Consequences	Potential Intangible Consequences
Ram ship in port with IED	Several hundred fatalities and injuries	Tens of millions of dollars for repair or loss of ferry[a]	*Loss of human capital*
Suicide dive bomber or limpet mine attack		Life and injury compensation: tens to hundreds of millions[b]	Changes in individual consumption
Standoff mortar or grenade launcher attack	Tens of fatalities and injuries	Costs of increased security: hundreds of millions[c]	
Suicide bombing on ship		*Cost of response[d]* *Increased insurance rates*	

[a] American Public Transportation Association (2006).

[b] Based on "Insurance Claims to Exceed $110m" (2004) and Knight and Pretty (1997) figures for previous ferry disasters, the amounts are likely to be in the high tens of millions to hundreds of millions, depending on the ratio of casualties to survivors. Also, according to Middle East Online, the Egyptian government is likely to pay nearly $26 million to the families of everyone who died in the February 3, 2006, disaster ("Egypt Government," 2006).

[c] The costs in increased security would likely be similar to those cited by Coughlin, Cohen, and Khan (2002) for the airline industry as ferries in the United States carry over 68 million passengers a year (U.S. Department of Transportation, 2000) and security would likely be stepped up from a relatively low present level in the event of a disaster.

[d] Bounding cost estimates have not been identified for items in italics.

Herald of Free Enterprise tragedy in Belgium, which caused 193 deaths ("Insurance Claims to Exceed $110m," 2004, p. 1; Knight and Pretty, 1997; Lawson and Weisbrod, 2005).

Similar to cruise ship attacks, land-based suicide terrorist strikes provide a measure for the expected consequences of martyr attacks on passenger ferries. As discussed in Chapter Five, based on the 652 suicide bombings in the RAND terrorism database, the median number of deaths and injuries associated with such incidents is 5 and 12, respectively. Assuming munitions of comparable size are used for standoff artillery attacks, the same range of consequences could also be expected for those scenarios.

Economic Consequences

The direct economic consequences of terrorist attacks on passenger ferries are the result of damage to the vessel. According to the American Public Transportation Association (2006), only one to two ferry boats are built every five years in the United States. Costs vary from about $250,000 for the smallest vessels up to tens of millions of dollars for the largest. Other economic consequences result from the resulting loss of life and the cost of immediate and continued response and change in policies following a terrorist attack.

Compensation for Injuries and Loss of Life

Various ferry accidents that have occurred indicate that fatalities and injuries from attacks on passenger ferries could expose owner-operators to large-scale compensation or liability payouts—either of which would have import for subsequent maritime insurance coverage. The 1994 sinking of the *Estonia* in the Baltic Sea (852 deaths), for instance, generated victim claims in excess of US$110 million while the (known) legal costs associated with the capsizing of the *Herald of Free Enterprise* outside the Belgian port of Zeebrugge in 1987 (193 fatalities) have been calculated at US$70 million ("Insurance Claims to Exceed $110m," 2004, p. 1; Knight and Pretty, 1997; Lawson and Weisbrod, 2005).

Increased Security Costs

Ferry attacks could also promote shifts in security policy, resulting in the largest economic effect of terrorist attacks on passenger ferries. In the Philippines, for instance, the 2004 strike against *SuperFerry 14* had a profound effect on perceived domestic terrorist threat contingencies and was a central factor in subsequent moves that have been made to deploy sea marshals on all ships traveling in Philippine waters as well as promulgate heightened surveillance, investigation, arrest, and detention powers for the police and intelligence services.[8] Attempts to

---

8   Comments made during the "Terrorism in Southeast Asia—The Threat and Response" conference, Singapore, April 12–13, 2006.

introduce extrajudicial measures of this sort[9] are noteworthy in light of the country's relatively recent martial past under Ferdinand Marcos and the extreme sensitivity this experience fostered—both within the governing establishment and among the population at large—toward sanctioning any type of extrajudicial processes or legal practices.

Increased security costs following terrorist attacks on ferries could reach hundreds of millions of dollars. As discussed in Chapter Five, increased costs for security for the airline industry provide a useful benchmark for comparison, with Coughlin, Cohen, and Khan (2002) estimating expenditures to be in the range of roughly $9 billion annually. Increased security after an attack would be much lower for the ferry industry than for the airline industry because it is a smaller system that moves fewer passengers. Comparing the approximately 66 million cruise passengers to the 685 million airline passengers, one would expect security in the cruise industry to be on the order of hundreds of millions of dollars, as opposed to billions.

Other Economic Consequences

Additional economic consequences would result from direct costs of response and potentially higher insurance rates following the terrorist events. Costs of response would include emergency response, medical and public health services, and decontamination as required. Changes in insurance rates would depend on the magnitude of damages and uptake rates of insurance prior to and following the terrorist events.

We have not yet identified reasonable estimates for bounding these sources of economic consequences.

Intangible Consequences

The principal intangible consequence of attacks on passenger ferries would involve their effects on individuals' consumption and invest-

---

[9] These measures are contained within a proposed antiterrorism bill, which at the time of writing, was still being debated in the legislature (anonymous Anti-Terrorism Task Force officials, 2005).

ment decisions in the future. Because ferry transit is such an important and visible part in some people's daily routines, these effects could lead to significant behavioral changes.

In the United States, ferry transit is largely a substitutable form of transportation. Following a terrorist attack, it could be expected that ridership would decline, but the economic costs of this shift would not necessarily be large.

However, in the United Kingdom, repeated acts of terrorism in the Dover Strait could encourage trucking companies to use the Chunnel as their primary conduit to the European continent. This underwater rail route, although rapid, is far more expensive than the sea crossing, which could potentially raise the overall rate-charge for freight shipments—creating a price burden that would ultimately fall on the individual consumer (anonymous UK customs and excise officials, 2005). Similarly, this effect may be particularly large in the developing world where geographic factors often dictate the need for cheap, high-volume passenger vessels to avail travel between island archipelagos as well as to compensate for the lack of viable surface infrastructure, such as a functioning road and bridge system (see Lawson and Weisbrod, 2005, p. 20). Even in advanced states, such considerations can have relevance. These economic and geographic pressures would seemingly decrease the extent of shifts in preferences for transportation and increase the economic consequences of decisions to use alternative transportation.

Passenger ferry attacks could also result in the loss of human capital to firms and society at large. Though this is difficult to quantify in economic terms, the scale of human consequences discussed above allows bounding of the potential impacts on human capital. As tragic as the loss of human life would be from these events, incidents that affect a few thousand passengers on a passenger ferry would not have a significant effect on the balance of skills and capabilities of a nation's workforce. Nevertheless, these consequences could be devastating to particular firms if a large proportion of the firm's skilled workforce were included in the hundreds or thousands of victims.

Risks of Terrorist Attacks on Passenger Ferries

We used the qualitative risk analysis methodology described in the appendix to assess the risks of terrorist attacks on cruise ships in terms of the threats, vulnerabilities, and consequences of these attack scenarios.

Threat of terrorist attack on passenger ferries is determined by both terrorists' intent and capability. As discussed previously, passenger vessels do not represent symbolic targets for terrorist attack. However, the scenarios considered are all ones that could capture media attention and result in both loss of life and economic damage. Thus, attack scenarios involving passenger ferries seem moderately aligned with terrorist intentions discussed in Chapter Two.

At the same time, some attack scenarios are more easily completed than others. While a suicide bombing would require only basic skills typical of volunteers, parasitic bombs would necessitate far more specialized maritime combat techniques and expertise. Capabilities required for other attack types would fall between these two extremes. Ramming a ship with an IED would require the military skill required to assemble a more sophisticated IED and firing and aiming a mortar (or other similar device) would require expert military skills associated with targeting weapons. As seen in Figure 6.1, this results in a matrix of passenger ferry attack scenarios that are moderate in terms of intent, spanning a broad range of capabilities.

The estimated likelihood of attack depends on both the threat posed by terrorists and the vulnerability of the chosen targets. As shown in Figure 6.2, threats to passenger ferries range from relatively high for on-board bomb and USS *Cole*–style IED attacks to relatively low for scenarios like those involving parasitic bombs, which require more advanced capabilities.[10]

The vulnerability of ferries to the attack scenarios considered falls into two categories. As discussed above, ferries must necessarily be

---

[10] The assessment of threat is based on the normalized, multiplicative combination of intent and capability assessments, as discussed in the appendix.

Figure 6.1
Assessment of the Capability Required in Scenarios Involving Terrorist Attacks on Passenger Ferries and Extent to Which the Scenario Aligns with Terrorist Groups' Intentions

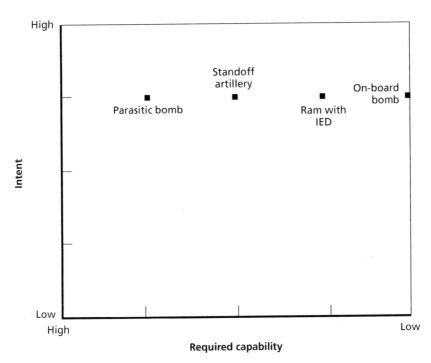

operated on a predictable schedule and in a manner that allows free and uninhibited access to large numbers of people. This makes this mode of public transport particularly vulnerable to scenarios involving suicide bombings or standoff artillery. Though security around ferries can be monitored and controlled while they are at dock, these vessels remain vulnerable to IED and parasitic bombing attacks. The predictability of their schedules in terms of arrival and departure times contributes to this vulnerability. Also, unlike cruise ships, passenger ferries are not designed to be as robust to partial failures of their hulls and would be more likely to sink if attacked. As Figures 6.3 and 6.4 show, the most likely attacks on passenger ferries (taking into account both threat and

Figure 6.2
Assessment of the Threat of Terrorist Attacks on Passenger Ferries and the Vulnerability of Passenger Ferries to These Attack Scenarios

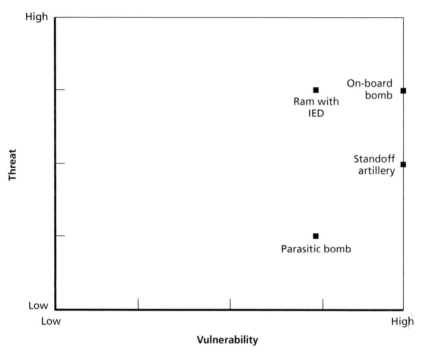

vulnerability) appear to manifest as on-board bombings and USS *Cole*–style attacks. The least likely appear to be those involving parasitic devices.

Finally, to determine the relative risk of various terrorist attacks on passenger ferries, one needs to consider both the likelihood of the assault in question and the potential consequences that might arise from it.[11]

Attack scenarios involving on-board bombs and USS *Cole*–style IED attacks on passenger ferries appear to be relatively high as compared to other maritime terrorism scenarios discussed in this book.

---

[11] The assessment of likelihood is based on the normalized, multiplicative combination of threat and vulnerability assessments, as discussed in the appendix.

Figure 6.3
Assessment of the Relative Likelihood of Terrorist Attacks on Passenger Ferries and Potential Economic Consequences of These Attack Scenarios

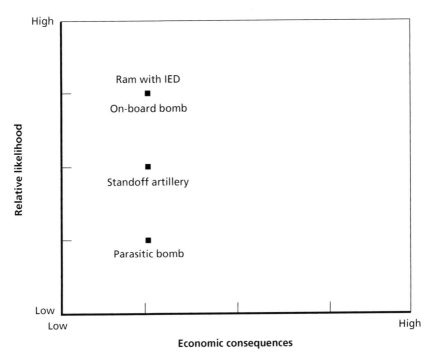

RAND *MG520-6.3*

They represent scenarios to which ferries are vulnerable and terrorists are seemingly motivated to conduct. The factor that most differentiates likelihood is capability. Scenarios involving on-board bombs would appear the easiest to conduct. On the other hand, there is much less variation on the range of expected consequences arising from each of the postulated contingencies assessed in this case study.

As discussed previously, the primary determinants of economic consequences of terrorist attacks on passenger ships are the costs of increased security that might be implemented following such assaults. Compared to other terrorist scenarios, in particular those involving container shipping, the economic effects of attacks on passenger

Figure 6.4
Assessment of the Relative Likelihood of Terrorist Attacks on Passenger
Ferries and Potential Human Consequences of These Attack Scenarios

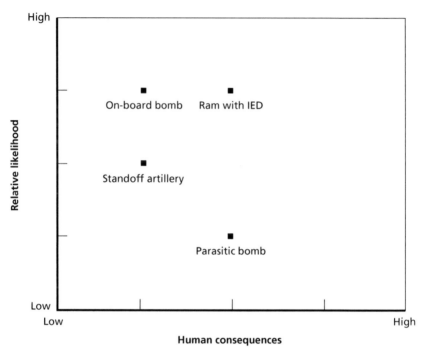

ferries can be expected to be relatively modest, though still in the order of hundreds of millions of dollars.

The potential human consequences are similarly consistent across scenarios and generally fall into two categories: (1) attacks involving small explosives or munitions and (2) attacks employing larger munitions, which could potentially sink the ship and kill hundreds of people.

Figures 6.3 and 6.4 summarize the risk to the passenger ferry scenarios covered in this chapter. They show that while the probability of attacks on passenger ferries is seemingly high, the potential consequences of the attacks are likely to be moderate. In this regard, assaults involving on-board bombing or standoff artillery are the most likely of the scenarios considered. When considering economic consequences, they are accordingly the scenarios of greatest risk since economic consequences are not expected to vary dramatically across these scenarios. However, from the perspective of human consequences, attacks involving IEDs or parasitic devices present a risk more comparable to those from standoff artillery because they have the potential to kill more people than do the other scenarios.

CHAPTER SEVEN

Risks of Maritime Terrorism Attacks Against Container Shipping

The intermodal shipping system is a critical component of international trade. The system of ocean routes, road, and rail networks connects almost any two points in the world. Traveling on specialized ocean vessels, truck chassis, and rail cars, container transport is inexpensive, reliable, and ubiquitous. The rise of container transportation over the past half century has enabled production to occur far from the goods' eventual market, and manufacturing to be partitioned into discrete steps, with work in progress traveling among production centers according to tightly choreographed schedules.

Today, approximately 112,000 merchant vessels, 6,500 ports and harbor facilities, and 45,000 shipping bureaus constitute the contemporary international maritime transport system, linking roughly 225 coastal nations, dependent territories, and island states. This network caters to around 80 percent of commercial freight, which, in 2001, included an estimated 15 million containers that collectively registered 232 million point-to-point movements across the world's seas.[1]

It is feared that terrorists could use the ubiquitous, anonymous, and largely innocuous steel boxes and their transport system to devastating effect (Flynn, 2004a). Global commerce relies on the predictable performance of the container supply chain, and a significant disruption at a critical facility—a channel, port, or exchange point—could disable for some time all business that relies on goods shipped through it. For

---

[1] Anonymous Maritime Intelligence Group analyst (2005). See also Herbert-Burns (2005, pp. 158–159), Sinai (2004, p. 49), Organization for Economic Cooperation and Development (2003), Central Intelligence Agency (undated).

example, over 40 percent of all containerized inputs into the United States pass through the ports of Los Angeles and Long Beach. A major disruption at these ports could damage the U.S. economy. Terrorists could also use the container supply chain to deliver a CBRN weapon to any location in the United States through a Trojan horse–style attack.

This chapter provides an overview of the nature and magnitude of risks from terrorist attacks via the container supply chain. The five scenarios listed below represent a range of threats within the two attack scenarios described above. The scenarios demonstrate the diversity of threats, vulnerabilities, and potential consequences of terrorist attack on container shipping:

- *Sinking a ship in a port of channel*: A ship is sunk or disabled in a narrow channel or port entrance in an effort to disrupt freight transportation. There are many scenarios for how this might be attempted including use of an on-board bomb, a USS *Cole* and M/V *Limburg*–style attack, or by having a diver place an explosive device on the hull of the ship.
- *Hijacking a ship*: Terrorists board and commandeer a ship with the intent of ramming it into a facility, bridge, or other structure to cause potential freight disruptions, attract media attention, and kill and injure civilians.
- *Detonating a nuclear bomb*: A container is used to transport a nuclear device into a port or near a city where it is detonated upon arrival. The container may arrive at its destination where it is detonated on a ship or via truck or rail.
- *Detonating a dirty bomb*: A container is used to transport a radiological device into a port or near a city where it is detonated upon arrival. The container may arrive at its destination where it is detonated on an inbound ship, or via an outbound truck or train. The amount of high explosives in this scenario is relatively small, and the consequences are due to the radiological contamination and response.[2]

---

[2] This is the scenario considered by Gordon et al. (2005).

- *Detonating a conventional bomb*: A container is used to transport a high-explosive device into a port or near a city where it is detonated upon arrival. The container may arrive at its destination where it is detonated on a ship or via truck or rail.

Attractiveness of Container Shipping as a Target of Terrorism

The container supply chain has been the focus of considerable attention, largely because it is widely seen to represent a viable conduit for availing the covert movement of terrorist weapons and personnel then facilitating an attack (anonymous former defense intelligence official, 2005). There are at least three factors that underscore this perceived attractiveness.

First, the container shipping system is an easy target. For terrorists, to attack or to use the container shipping system appears to be low risk. The container supply chain is very accessible and operationally flexible. These attributes have contributed to the development of a highly vibrant and efficient global import-export transportation network and have also created openings for terrorist misuse and exploitation. Because container transportation is critical to the U.S. and global economies, security measures cannot have a significant effect on the movement of goods; most experts acknowledge that inspecting all or even a significant fraction of incoming cargo without adversely affecting commerce would be extremely difficult and expensive. Currently, between 2 and 5 percent of containers are currently checked at ports around the world, even at facilities equipped with the most advanced x-ray or gamma ray scanning technologies.[3] Since relatively few containers are scanned or inspected, it is feared that terrorists could easily employ the system for their ends.

---

[3] Anonymous Department of Homeland Security Liaison attache (Singapore) (2005). See also Frittelli (2004, p. 4), Raymond (2005, p. 187), Brew (2003, p. 5), and Customs and Border Protection (2004).

Second, the container shipping system is pervasive and ubiquitous; it is able to transport efficiently a weapon of mass destruction to any location in the world. The intermodal shipping container is a common sight. Were a bomb to be shipped via a container and get past the gates of the port, it would travel along an open highway and rail network that is optimized to transport goods quickly and efficiently. A location-sensing device in the container could be programmed to detonate the weapon when it reaches an area with a dense population.

Third, a successful attack on the container shipping system could inflict significant economic damage on the nation. Ports are critical components of the global supply chain and the principal location where containers make the switch between ocean and land transport. Were a bomb to destroy a port or disable a vessel in a critical access channel, the operations of that port would be disrupted severely. The U.S. freight transport system operates at its capacity, so a disruption at a single port would be felt throughout the system. In addition, ports are typically located in densely populated areas, so the explosion of a weapon of mass destruction at a port also has the ability to cause many deaths.

Vulnerabilities of the Container Shipping System to Terrorism

The container supply chain is ubiquitous, creating many opportunities for terrorist infiltration. Container ships carry goods and commodities from hundreds of companies and individuals, which, in most cases, are transported and received from inland warehouses. Every shipment involves many actors: the exporter, the importer, the freight forwarder, a customs broker, excise inspectors, truckers, railroad workers, dock workers, and the crews of feeder and ocean vessels (Willis and Ortiz, 2004). Whenever and wherever a container is handled during movement represents a potential vulnerability for the security and integrity of the cargo. Terrorists may exploit vulnerabilities to "stuff" a container with a weapon or tamper with its contents (Frittelli, 2004, p. 9; Hoge and Rose, 2001, p. 188).

There are several ways by which container shipping could be used to facilitate terrorist designs, ranging from availing the covert movement of arms to assisting with smuggling operatives into a third country.[4] Consider the case of a radiological dispersion device, i.e., a "dirty bomb," that is detonated at a U.S. port. Such a device need not kill many people to have a significant economic effect. Gordon et al. (2005) report that two small radiological dispersal devices, each containing 5 pounds of high explosives could contaminate an area of 5–10 km². Depending on the amount of radioactive material contained in the device and placement of the device within the port, this could require closure of significant parts of a large port for weeks or months, if not years. Rosoff and von Winterfeldt (2005) noted that closures of several months could be prompted by detonation of a device constructed using radioactive pellets from a blood or industrial irradiator in a U.S. facility (representing 10,000 to 100,000 Ci of radioactive material).

Terrorist attacks of the containerized shipping system are more likely to exploit the cargo supply chain than to attack the vessels carrying the cargo. Container ships are large vessels with considerable freeboard; a significant quantity of explosives would be required to sink the vessel. Also, to place a bomb in a container with the intent of sinking the vessel requires that the compromised container be loaded into the appropriate location on the vessel; the would-be terrorist would have no control over this aspect of the attack. Ocean transport is not a concern of most citizens. Therefore, such an attack would elicit little

---

[4] Commercial shipping represents a tried and tested means of moving people around the world without being detected. Illegal migrants have frequently been able to enter a third country by posing as sailors, which gives them the right to go ashore (while their vessel is docked) without being subjected to the type of immigration procedures that are used to check normal passengers. Terrorists could certainly exploit this modus operandi to facilitate the placement of their own cadres around the world. Of more immediate relevance to container carriers is the possibility of an operative stowing away in an on-board crate. One case just after September 11, which involved an Egyptian who had transformed an empty container bound for Halifax, Nova Scotia, into a sophisticated living area complete with a bed, food-making facilities, and a rudimentary latrine system, highlights the potential. The individual, who was apprehended in possession of American airport maps and security passes, disappeared after being granted bail (anonymous Control Risks Group [UK] personnel, 2005). See also Sinai (2004, p. 57) and Shenon (2003).

attention and most likely evoke little "terror." An exception would be an attack that sinks or disables a vessel in a canal or strait, disrupting maritime trade. However, there are few nonsubstitutable choke points; for example, bypassing the Malacca Strait requires three days of additional travel. Were the Panama and Suez canals to be disabled, it is possible to route traffic around South America and Africa. Transport costs would rise and delays would increase, but the overall effects would be marginal. Other than oil, highly perishable food, and critical medical supplies, most commodities would not be affected significantly by short delays in delivery (anonymous Lloyd's of London analysts, 2005).

Were containers themselves secure, the vulnerabilities associated with their packing and movement would be mitigated; unfortunately, the locks and seals used to secure containers are rudimentary and easily defeated. Existing devices offer little, if any, protection, and often consist of nothing more than a bolt that can be quickly cut and reattached.[5] A standard seal purchased in bulk may cost as little as a few cents. More-secure tamper-resistant and tamper-evident seals may cost up to several dollars each. The most robust container security devices, which include GPS transponders and radio frequency identification (RFID) devices that transmit data regarding the integrity of the container, may cost several hundred dollars. Most commercial shipping companies have been reluctant to deploy the more sophisticated seals, citing cost as the principal concern. At the time of writing, the international maritime industry has not embraced any of these devices.[6]

The vulnerabilities extend to the level of the package. The Trans International Routier (TIR) haulage system is used to transport merchandise from warehouse to port; any container bearing the TIR logo is assumed to have been inspected and sealed by relevant authorities. The TIR designation precludes any additional inspection before stuffing into a container and loading onto a vessel. Terrorists could compromise this internationally recognized arrangement and exploit it for their own purposes in at least three ways:

---

[5]   See, for instance, Saunders (2003, p. 4).

[6]   Anonymous International Maritime Bureau personnel (2005). In bulk order form, these types of technologies would cost at least US$500 per container.

- bribe or co-opt authorities to issue a TIR designation for a package or container containing a weapon
- commandeer a TIR-certified container; break the rudimentary seal; stuff the cargo with weapons, explosives, or other material; and reseal the container before it is transferred from shore to ship
- forge a TIR stamp and documentation for their cargo (anonymous former defense intelligence official, 2005).

The effectiveness of point-of-origin inspections for containerized freight is questionable. Many littoral states fail to vet stevedores,[7] do not require that truck drivers present valid identification before entering the port, and overlook the need to ensure that an accurate manifest accompany all cargo.[8] Standards for inspecting containers at originating ports do not exist. It is exceptionally difficult, and often impossible, to inspect containers en route. Inspections at U.S. seaports may occur too late to prevent a terrorist attack. The ISPS code alleviates some of these problems by mandating a minimum set of requirements to govern the integrity of the maritime export-import chain.[9] How-

---

[7] This is true of both small and large terminals. Privacy regulations in the Netherlands, for instance, preclude the option of comprehensive security vetting for dock workers without first gaining their permission. In the words of one Dutch expert: "I would be amazed if harbor employees at Rotterdam, Antwerp or Amsterdam were required to undergo any form of mandatory background criminal check" (anonymous Control Risks Group [Netherlands] personnel, 2005).

[8] Again, in many ways, this is a problem unique to small, resource-constrained littoral nations. Singapore, which runs arguably one of the world's most sophisticated and well-protected commercial maritime terminals, does not require shipping companies to declare goods on their vessels if they are only transiting through the country's port (largely due to a fear that, if this was made mandatory, the resulting red tape would deflect trade north to Malaysia). As a result, the government does not know what is being transported on the vast bulk of carriers that transship through the city state (anonymous Ministry of Foreign Affairs officials and Raytheon and Glenn Defense Marine analysts, 2005).

[9] The ISPS was adopted by the International Maritime Organization (IMO) at its December 2002 conference. The ISPS outlines minimum security procedures that all ships and ports must meet to improve overall maritime security. Any vessel that does not meet these requirements or which leaves from a port that does not can be turned away by relevant authorities at the destination terminal. Stipulations in the code are based on those that

ever, the ISPS does not cover small vessels nor operations in coastal rivers and tributaries. Furthermore, most oceanic trading countries have failed to meet these regulations[10] and many nations do not audit security measures that have been enacted. One analyst observed that security practices at Rotterdam—one of the world's busiest commercial ocean terminals—remain weak, constituting not much more than "a tick in the box exercise" (anonymous Control Risks Group [Netherlands] personnel, 2005).

Potential Consequences of Terrorist Attacks on the Container Shipping System

Human Consequences

The human consequences of attacks on the container shipping system range from minimal for direct attacks using conventional weapons to massive for an attack using a nuclear bomb.

Should terrorists sink or disable a ship in a channel or port, hijack the vessel for use as a ram to destroy infrastructure, or plant a conventional bomb on a container ship, the human consequences are bounded by the number of persons on the vessel and in the immediate vicinity. Twenty-four crew members operate a vessel capable of transporting more than 3,000 40-foot containers.[11] Therefore, the maximum number of injuries or deaths resulting from an attack on a vessel is in the tens. In the case in which terrorists hijack a vessel and use it destructively, the injuries and deaths affect all persons in the path of the vessel. In a worst-case scenario, the injuries and deaths would reach into the hundreds.

---

underscore MTSA. For further details, see Frittelli (2004, pp. 13–14), "FAQ on ISPS Code and Maritime Security" (undated).

[10] As of June 2004, only 10 percent of port facilities around the world were in compliance with ISPS stipulations. See "ISPS Code Status Update 01" (undated).

[11] Pollak (2004). Also, the *Regina Maersk*, a post-Panamax container ship that entered service in 1996, operates with only 15 crew (see Maersk Line, undated).

When a container is used to transport a conventional weapon, the human consequences depend on the location of the container when the weapon is detonated. For example, if the container is in midtown Manhattan on a weekday morning when the bomb it carries detonates, the loss of life will be significantly greater than that if the container were sitting in an intermodal transfer facility at a port during off hours. In this study, we consider only the consequences of detonation at a port. The human consequences of the detonation of a conventional weapon in a shipping container are likely to be similar to those of the case in which a vessel is used destructively, depending on the configuration of the port area and its proximity to areas of dense human activity.

Radiological and nuclear weapons have the capability of inflicting direct and severe human consequences. Since U.S. ports are equipped with radiation portal monitors, we assume that the detonation of a radiological device or nuclear bomb would occur at or near the seaport of entry. An artifact of U.S. industrialization, ports tend to be near cities, so the detonation of a radiological device or nuclear bomb near a port has the potential to affect or kill many people. For the detonation of a radiological device, depending on the size and placement of a bomb as well as atmospheric conditions, the injuries and deaths resulting from such an attack range from tens to hundreds (Rosoff and von Winterfeldt, 2005). Abt Associates estimated the range of deaths from the detonation of a Hiroshima-sized, 10–20-kiloton nuclear bomb at a U.S. port to be 50,000 to 1 million persons, depending on the method of detonation, the density of the area, and the path of the fallout. Since some illness and fatalities associated with exposure to radiation can occur in the form of latent cancer, the consequences may persist for decades.[12]

---

[12] Abt (2003). Note that if terrorists constructed a device smaller than 10 kT, the resulting detonation would have a smaller destructive radius. However, depending on the type of detonation and location of the detonation its consequences may be comparable in terms of fatalities and economic damage.

Economic Consequences

The economic consequences of a successful terrorist attack on the container shipping system are likely to be large and widespread. This is in contrast to human casualties, which are large only in the event of a successful attack with a weapon of mass destruction. Economic consequences of attacks on the container shipping system may be parsed into direct and indirect effects. The direct effects are an immediate consequence of the terrorist attack: life and injury compensation, repair or replacement of the vessel (if terrorists attack a container ship), losses of cargo, and damaged and destroyed private property and public infrastructure. Indirect effects are a consequence of the role of the container supply chain in the economy: short-term business disruptions due to delayed or missing shipments, long-term adjustments to the modified freight transport system, augmented security procedures and equipment, and lost revenue to the government and firms. Because the container shipping system is interwoven into the economy, quantifying the economic consequences of a terrorist attack on the container shipping system is especially difficult. Therefore, we provide an order-of-magnitude estimate of direct and indirect economic consequences. We do not consider some types of economic effects because of a lack of reliable data on which to base estimates: the direct costs of response and recovery and the indirect costs of increased insurance premiums and changes in investment patterns.

Human consequences, quantified in the previous section, result in economic consequences proportional to the number of lives lost or injuries incurred. Based on past incidents and analyses of possible terrorist attacks, we estimate the economic consequences per death or injury to be approximately $1 million.[13] Therefore, in the cases in which a ship is attacked or hijacked, the worst-case economic consequences due to life and injury compensation range from tens of millions of dollars for

---

[13] "Insurance Claims to Exceed $110m" (2004) and Knight and Pretty (1997) quantify the amounts insured for in the 1987 *Herald of Free Enterprise* (193 dead) and 1994 *Estonia* (852 dead) ferry disasters as $70M and $110M, respectively. Both of these figures are thought to be somewhat underestimated, as these are only the known claims. The typical known compensation per death for these incidents ranges from $130,000 to $360,000. Abt (2003) estimated compensation to be $3 million per death.

the bombing of a ship to hundreds of millions of dollars for the hijacking of a vessel. For cases in which the container is used to facilitate an attack, life and injury compensation is estimated to be hundreds of millions of dollars for an attack via a conventional bomb, hundreds of millions of dollars for a dirty bomb attack, and hundreds of billions of dollars for a nuclear attack.

Damage to property and infrastructure in a port area represents direct effects of a terrorist attack on the containerized shipping system. For an attack on a vessel, the damage will be limited to the vessel itself and will cost tens of millions of dollars to repair or replace (Thompson and Fry, 2004). If all of the cargo on the vessel is lost, the economic consequences may be in the hundreds of millions of dollars (Thompson and Fry, 2004). Ports are key pieces of public infrastructure and an attack may seek to destroy the ability of the port to operate efficiently. For example, two key bridges service the ports of Los Angeles and Long Beach; the replacement value of each is approximately $50 million (Gordon et al., 2005). Therefore, infrastructure damage from a terrorist attack is likely to be in the tens of millions of dollars. When the container is used to transport the weapon, damage to the port, its facilities, and surrounding area will occur, but the extent may vary widely depending on the type of bomb. In a conventional bomb attack, assuming that a critical piece of infrastructure—such as a bridge—is not damaged, infrastructure damage is likely to be in the millions of dollars;[14] in the previously identified case of a dirty bomb attack using a small conventional explosive, the physical damage is posited to be minimal, on the order of several hundred thousand dollars (Gordon et al., 2005); and in an attack with a nuclear weapon, the port itself could conceivably be destroyed, resulting in billions of dollars of infrastructure damage.[15] Many businesses operate at U.S. ports and any attack is likely to destroy public property, including facilities, cranes, and handling equipment in addition to cargo. In an attack with a conventional

---

[14] We estimate that the damage in the area surrounding a bomb would be an order of magnitude less than that of a piece of critical infrastructure.

[15] The destruction wrought by a nuclear attack is likely to be an order of magnitude higher than the figure of $50 million per bridge cited by Gordon et al. (2005).

bomb, property damage may be relatively minor, in the billions of dollars; in an attack with a dirty bomb or a nuclear weapon, much property may be contaminated or destroyed, with economic effects ranging from tens of millions to hundreds of billions of dollars; a nuclear bomb is likely to destroy or contaminate homes and businesses in the vicinity of the port (Gordon et al., 2005).

Significant economic costs would occur if a successful terrorist attack were to disable a critical U.S. port for a long period.[16] The result of any successful attack is likely to be the immediate closure of the attacked port—regardless of actual damage—and may instigate a shutdown of the U.S. intermodal transportation system until the system could be determined to be secure (anonymous Department of Homeland Security Liaison attaches, 2005). So critical is the system to the operation of the economy that former U.S. Coast Guard officer and researcher at the Council on Foreign Relations Stephen Flynn believes that the immediate and latent economic effects from such a terrorist attack on the container supply chain could lead to a global recession.[17]

The closure of all 29 seaports along the U.S. West Coast in October 2002 provides an empirical indication of the damage that could occur from the shutdown of a key seaport. From September 27 to October 9, 2002, port owners and operators locked the gates of their facilities along the U.S. West Coast, shutting them down for business. The ports on the U.S. West Coast are critical to U.S. trade: the ports of Los Angeles and Long Beach are the entry point for over 40 percent of U.S.-bound containers; terminals in Washington handle approximately 42 percent of that state's maritime imports and exports by value. The lockout disrupted the itineraries of more than 200 ships carrying 300,000 containers, resulting in cargo delays, costly diversions to alternative ports, and unemployment lines as businesses laid off workers and cut production. The cost to the U.S. economy—in the form of delayed shipments and business disruptions—has been estimated

---

[16] Since U.S. ports are to be equipped with radiation portal monitors, we assume that, in the estimation of economic effects, a radiological device or nuclear weapon is detected at the port and that detonation occurs at the port.

[17] Flynn (2004b, p. 25); see also Chalk et al. (2005, p. 34).

to range from $450 million to several billion dollars; the subsequent effort to clear freight backlogs is thought to have removed between 0.4 and 1.1 percent of nominal GDP from prominent Asian exporters, including Hong Kong, Malaysia, and Singapore. It is worth noting that the lockout necessitated very few post-strike changes that would slow supply, unlike what might be expected following a terrorist attack (Richardson, 2004, p. 66; Organization for Economic Cooperation and Development, 2003, pp. 17–18; Department of Foreign Affairs and Trade, 2003).

Again, we provide order-of-magnitude estimates for indirect economic costs of an attack on the container shipping system. The Congressional Budget Office recently estimated that an unexpected one-week shutdown of the ports of Los Angeles and Long Beach would have a short-term macroeconomic effect ranging from $65 million to $150 million per day (Arnold, 2006). Since we expect a brief shutdown of the port in the event of an attack on a vessel or a conventional bomb, the short-term business disruptions would therefore be in the billions of dollars. National business disruptions from a dirty-bomb attack that closes the ports of Los Angeles and Long Beach for several months have been estimated to be in the tens of billions of dollars.[18] In the short-term, e.g., periods shorter than one year—the detonation of a nuclear weapon would cause a similar amount of business disruption as would a dirty bomb. Long-term disruptions to the freight transport system would result from any attack on the container shipping system, with economic consequences.

In all cases, security procedures would be tightened. Since September 11, 2001, expenditures on port security have been several billion dollars; in response to an attack on a U.S. port, we estimate that expenditures would double, and direct costs of additional security procedures and equipment would remain in the billions of dollars.[19]

---

[18] Gordon et al. (2005) estimated the broader economic effects of a dirty-bomb attack that shuts down the ports of Los Angeles and Long Beach for 120 days to be $34 billion.

[19] See the U.S. Department of Homeland Security budget for FY 2006 (U.S. Department of Homeland Security, 2006).

Intangible Consequences

Our estimates of the intangible consequences of a terrorist attack on a major U.S. port, though speculative, are derived from the human and economic effects. All attacks result in the loss of human capital—the experience and skills of workers. Some affected firms might be unable to cope with the loss. Most of the attack scenarios that we consider do not result in significant loss of life or economic damage; intangible consequences of these types of attacks are fundamentally political in nature. The responses of politicians might be to impose stricter guidelines on the movement of container freight. The intangible consequences of a successful attack with a weapon of mass destruction would be political and social upheaval, possibly resulting in political and economic instability.

A successful terrorist attack on a vessel would have political ramifications that may lead to economic consequences. As discussed previously, if terrorists were successful in sinking or disabling a vessel in a channel, or hijacking a vessel and using it to destroy infrastructure, the loss of life and local economic damage would be relatively small. However, since the container shipping system and port security have received considerable attention, the public would perceive the attack as a failure of leadership and our current policies. Taking the experience of aviation security after the attacks of September 11, 2001, as an example, decisionmakers would react most likely to the event by greatly increasing waterborne patrols of port areas and increased inspection of vessels entering U.S. territorial waters.

Alternatively, if the attack takes the form of a bomb being transported by a container, the intangible consequences would be different. As discussed earlier, the direct human and economic consequences would be minor from a national standpoint. The public and certain decisionmakers would view the attack as verification of the danger that the container shipping system poses to the United States. The result would be the quick implementation of increased scanning and inspection of containers, with direct effects on the U.S. economy.

The most significant damage would result from a successful attack on U.S. soil via a weapon of mass destruction, especially a nuclear bomb, shipped via a container. Such an attack would be beyond the ability of local and state agencies to respond and would create a humanitarian disaster of an enormous magnitude. The intangible consequences would be the loss of human capital in a wide area. Also, similar to the reaction of the nation after Hurricane Katrina devastated New Orleans, the loss of an American city, its history and culture, would have profound effects.

Summary of Consequences

Table 7.1 summarizes the consequences of successful terrorist attacks for the scenarios discussed in the previous section. We have not attempted to estimate costs associated with terms in italics.

A nuclear strike could conceivably destroy a port, and even more rudimentary radiological strikes have the potential to impede a terminal's operations seriously over the long term should they result in large-scale radioactive contamination. In time, the supply chain would adapt to the loss of a port with increases in capacity elsewhere in the system. The Congressional Budget Office estimated that a three-year shutdown of the ports of Los Angeles and Long Beach would result in macroeconomic losses of $45 billion to $70 billion per year (Arnold, 2006). Therefore, in the case of a nuclear attack, which would close a port for at least several years, the macroeconomic effects would be in the hundreds of billions of dollars. For the case of an attack with a dirty bomb, the length of the shutdown would be much less, and the macroeconomic effects would be on the order of tens of billions of dollars.

Risks of Terrorist Attacks on Container Shipping

The risk of terrorist attacks on or using the container shipping system may be assessed by integrating the threat, vulnerability, and consequences discussed in the previous sections. We apply the qualitative risk assessment methodology discussed in the appendix.

The assessment of intent and capability of attack gives an indication of the relative threat of a particular type of attack. Figure 7.1 presents the results of the qualitative assessment of intent and capability for container attack scenarios. Nuclear detonation scenarios represent

Table 7.1
Potential Consequences of Terrorist Attack Scenarios Involving Container Shipping

Maritime Terrorism Scenario	Potential Human Consequences	Potential Economic Consequences	Potential Intangible Consequences
Sink or disable a ship in a channel or at port	Up to tens of injuries and deaths of crew	Tens of millions of dollars in life and injury compensation Tens of millions of dollars to repair or replace ship Hundreds of millions of dollars in lost cargo Billions of dollars in short-term business disruptions Billions of dollars in augmented security procedures *Changes in firm investment* *Increased insurance rates*	*Loss of human capital* *Changes in consumer patterns of consumption*
Hijack ship and use to destroy infrastructure	Up to hundreds of injuries and deaths of crew; several hundred civilian casualties	Same as for sinking or disabling a vessel Hundreds of millions of dollars in life and injury compensation Tens of millions of dollars in damaged infrastructure	*Loss of human capital* *Changes in consumer patterns of consumption*
Use shipping container as a delivery device for a conventional bomb	Several hundred injuries and deaths	Hundreds of millions of dollars in life and injury compensation Millions of dollars in damaged infrastructure Millions of dollars in destroyed property Billions of dollars in short-term business disruptions Billions of dollars in augmented security procedures *Cost of response and recovery* *Changes in firm investment* *Increased insurance rates*	Loss of human capital

the highly emotive, high consequence types of attacks that correspond well with terrorist intentions discussed in Chapter Two. However, the required capability to conduct this type of scenario is also the most demanding. Sinking or disabling a ship and and hijacking a ship also required special skills related to knowledge of ship design or piloting a

Table 7.1—Continued

Maritime Terrorism Scenario	Potential Human Consequences	Potential Economic Consequences	Potential Intangible Consequences
Use shipping container as a delivery device for a radiological dispersion device	Tens to hundreds of injuries and deaths	Hundreds of millions of dollars in life and injury compensation Hundreds of thousands of dollars in contaminated or damaged infrastructure Millions of dollars in contaminated or damaged property Tens of billions of dollars in short-term business disruptions Billions of dollars in augmented security procedures Tens of billions of dollars in long-term macroeconomic effects *Cost of response and recovery* *Changes in firm investment* *Increased insurance rates*	*Loss of human capital* *Changes in consumer patterns of consumption* *Political consequences*
Use shipping container as a delivery device for a nuclear weapon	50,000– 1,000,000 deaths	Hundreds of billions of dollars in life and injury compensation Billions of dollars in damaged and contaminated infrastructure Hundreds of billions of dollars in damaged and contaminated property Tens of billions of dollars in short-term business disruptions Tens of billions of dollars in augmented security procedures Hundreds of billions of dollars in long-term macroeconomic effects *Cost of response and recovery* *Changes in firm investment* *Increased insurance rates*	*Loss of human capital* *Changes in consumer patterns of consumption* *Political consequences*

ship in a port or channel. A dirty bomb requires specialized knowledge of handling radioactive materials and building explosive devices with-effective dispersal capabilities. In contrast, building a container-sized conventional explosive device requires only basic military skills.

Figure 7.1
Assessment of the Capability Required in Scenarios Involving Terrorist Attacks on Container Shipping and Extent to Which the Scenario Aligns with Terrorist Groups' Intentions

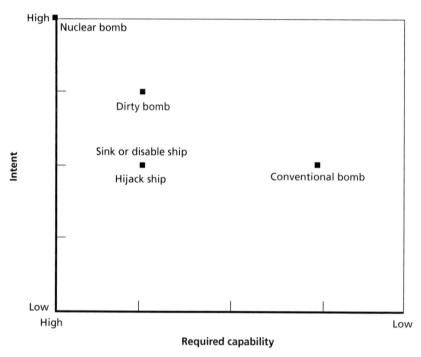

Taking intent and capability into account, relative threat of these scenarios is plotted in Figure 7.2.[20] This assessment suggests that all container shipping scenarios considered represent roughly equivalent threats except those involving nuclear detonation. Nuclear detonation scenarios represent a lower threat because of the high required capabilities.

Figure 7.2 presents assessments of relative vulnerabilities of each scenario. The container shipping system is relatively vulnerable. Access controls for the waterways surrounding ports are minimal. Access to the port terminals themselves requires some authentication, but since

---

[20] The assessment of threat is based on the normalized, multiplicative combination of intent and capability assessments, as discussed in the appendix.

Figure 7.2
Assessment of the Threat of Terrorist Attacks on Container Shipping and the Vulnerability of Container Shipping to These Attack Scenarios

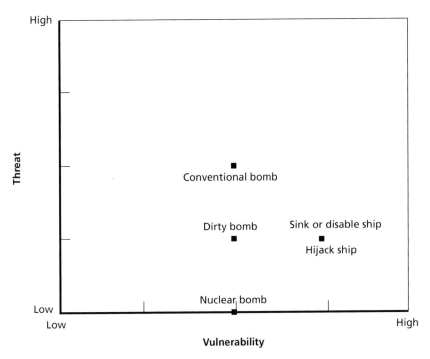

RAND MG520-7.2

these facilities are designed to facilitate commerce, the entry and exit controls are not too stringent. Therefore, using the qualitative risk assessment methodology in the appendix, we determined that the relatively likelihood of the attack scenarios that we consider is greatest for a hijacking or attempt at sinking or disabling a ship, in which the terrorists would approach a vessel from an open waterway. In contrast, container shipping is somewhat less vulnerable to scenarios involving placing a device in a container because of security procedures in place to restrict access to containers during stuffing, reviewing manifests, and inspecting containers.

The assessment of threat and vulnerability gives an indication of the relatively likelihood of a particular type of attack.[21] Comparing the relative likelihood of an attack and the consequences gives an indication of the overall risk posed by a particular type of attack. Figures 7.3 and 7.4 present likelihood versus consequences in terms of economic damages and human impacts, respectively. The consequence assessments used are based on the discussions above and Table 7.1.

Once again, the only distinction made among these scenarios is that the scenario involving nuclear detonation is less likely than the

Figure 7.3
Assessment of the Relative Likelihood of Terrorist Attacks on Container Shipping and Potential Economic Consequences of These Attack Scenarios

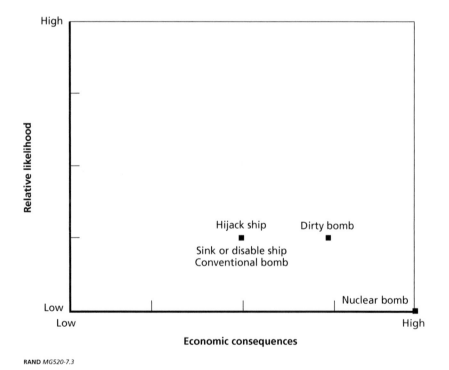

RAND *MG520-7.3*

---

[21] The assessment of likelihood is based on the normalized, multiplicative combination of threat and vulnerability assessments, as discussed in the appendix.

Figure 7.4
Assessment of the Relative Likelihood of Terrorist Attacks on Container Shipping and Potential Human Consequences of These Attack Scenarios

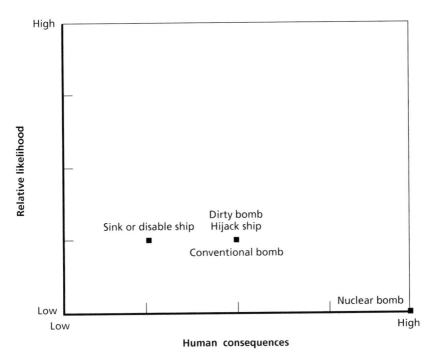

RAND MG520-7.4

others. As a group of scenarios, these are overall less likely than those involving ferries and cruise ships.

Because of the reliance of the U.S. and global economies on the intermodal shipping system, the risk, in terms of economic consequences, of terrorist attacks that affect a port is generally greater than those that target a ship (i.e., hijacking or sinking or disabling a ship). In fact, a scenario involving a dirty-bomb detonation appears to be among the riskiest of those considered. In contrast, all scenarios appear to represent quite low risks in terms of human consequences because of the low likelihood of a nuclear detonation scenario and the relatively low consequences of most other scenarios.

With respect to human consequences, the worst-case scenarios we present estimate small human consequences for conventional attacks (disabling a vessel, hijacking a vessel, or destruction with a conventional bomb). Though relatively less likely, the potential human consequences of the delivery of a weapon of mass destruction via a shipping container increase the risk from such attacks.

CHAPTER EIGHT

Discussion

The aim of this book has been to address several aspects of maritime terrorism: (1) threat and vulnerability, (2) consequences, and (3) liability implications, particularly regarding attacks on passenger and container shipping. Threat, vulnerability, and consequences collectively define the risk profile with regard to different forms of potential attack: in essence, weighting the likelihood of an attack (given the capabilities and intent of known terrorist groups and the characteristics of potential targets) against the projected damage that such an attack might inflict. Some of the basic assumptions underlying these sorts of calculations are very intuitive. For example, other factors being equal, terrorists will tend to prefer easier, less costly attack strategies to complicated, more expensive ones. Likewise, attacks that cause more-significant damage, other factors being equal, will tend to be more invidious and burdensome to society as a whole. Threat and vulnerability information, when put together, allow for a qualified assessment of the relative attractiveness of different types of targets and attack modalities to terrorists.[1] Consequence assessment, on the other hand, involves constructing a footprint regarding all of the economic and intangible harms that might likely result from different forms of attack. Taken in

---

[1] We acknowledge that the assessment is necessarily nondefinitive, as terrorists frequently do not have sufficient or appropriate information to make a fully reasoned judgment of the pros and cons of attacking particular targets. In addition, other factors could conceivably shape the decisionmaking process of terrorists and move it away from a purely rationally driven cost/benefit analysis (for example, the value preferences or self-defined priorities of terrorists' leaders).

combination, threat, vulnerability, and consequences can suggest the relative magnitude of the risks to U.S. interests associated with different attack scenarios. This is potentially very useful information, given the need to prioritize limited resources in detection, prevention, and interdiction efforts.

Drawing on this framework for examining the risks posed by maritime terrorism, we conclude that some types of attack scenarios present considerably greater risks than others. For example, with regard to scenarios involving cruise ships, attacks employing on-board bombs appear more probable and, on the whole, pose greater risk than do attacks involving scuba-diving terrorists with limpet mines (which would require greater technical expertise and better logistics capability to execute). Similarly, scenarios involving on-board explosives attacks or USS *Cole*–style IED attacks against ferries are among the highest-risk scenarios we considered, in particular because ferries are characterized by prominent structural vulnerabilities, weak security measures, and close proximity to mass media outlets. Many plausible attacks on container shipping pose comparatively low risk, owing to the fact that container ships, as opposed to passenger ships, are intrinsically less attractive as targets: The opportunity to inflict high-profile human casualties aboard cargo ships is simply lower. On the other hand, an attack involving the use of a compromised cargo container as a concealed-weapon platform poses a greater risk than do attacks on the vessels themselves, in part because such an attack would leverage the vulnerabilities inherent to the container shipping system. Even so, the risk of a CBRN attack using a compromised cargo container is somewhat offset by the difficulty of terrorists' obtaining an unconventional weapon capacity in the first place. Nevertheless, the prospect of severe commercial disruptions or catastrophic damage associated with a CBRN attack boosts the risks (in terms of human and economic consequences) associated with this kind of maritime scenario.

This sort of calculus regarding relative risks posed by maritime terrorism scenarios raises the question of absolute risk: What is the risk in absolute terms connected with a particular type of attack, as compared with the full spectrum of potential terrorism risks? This is a very difficult question to answer. One way to begin to address it would be (1) to expand on the analysis that we have undertaken here and (2) to try to characterize threat, vulnerability, and consequences across a much broader range of potential attack modalities. But though this could help to answer part of the question regarding absolute risks (e.g., by characterizing the consequential "footprint" for a broader range of attacks), it cannot answer the question fully. In particular, any empirically based assessment of terrorism risks necessarily draws on past experience and current intelligence as a metric for estimating future probabilities. And as we have already discussed, growing concerns about the risks posed by maritime terrorism are fundamentally based not on the experience of past attacks, but rather on increased recognition of unexploited vulnerabilities, allegedly shifting intentions and capabilities among terrorist groups, and the potential for risk transformation effects as terrorist groups respond to increased vigilance and security measures on land. For current purposes, it suffices to say that the absolute risks associated with maritime attacks involving cruise ships, ferries, and cargo containers are not negligible; evaluating relative risk can help guide policymakers in formulating priorities for guarding against attacks in the future.

By contrast with the foregoing, our analysis of civil liability in connection with maritime terrorism addresses something qualitatively different from our analysis of terrorism risks. At heart, liability is a policy mechanism for responding to injuries and for shifting related costs from one party to another. Thus, liability can perhaps best be understood as one aspect of the government's *response* to terrorism. That response includes both a set of incentives for private-sector firms to take measures to prevent and mitigate attacks *ex ante* and a set of rules for shifting some of the costs of attacks away from victims and (potentially) to third-party commercial interests *ex post*. Liability is only one of several aspects of the government's *response* to terrorism, but it is a particularly important aspect of that response for several reasons. First, because civil liability operates as a cost-shifting mechanism, it contributes directly to the magnitude of financial risks that private-sector firms face in connection with future attacks. By corollary, liability provides a foundation for commercial insurance mechanisms that spread terrorism risks: In principle, firms have no incentive to insure against risks for which they carry no legal or financial responsibility. Second, civil liability involves a very complex system of rules for determining whether and to what extent the victims of particular maritime attacks will be compensable. Without understanding those rules, it becomes impossible to assess how the compensation of victims might work, or fail to work, in the future. Finally, the essential nature of the civil justice system involves the application of precedent, by analogy, to determine the outcome of future cases. That means that the contours of liability for terrorist acts may well grow out of legal rules that were originally developed to deal with other sorts of problems (e.g., responsibility for negligence or for the criminal acts of third parties). Whether *that* is likely to result in a reasonable basis for compensating terrorism victims or for structuring private-sector security incentives remains to be seen.

On an immediate level, our analysis of liability issues offers some specific insights with regard to the sequelae of future attacks on cruise ships, ferries, and containerized shipping. Thus, as a threshold matter, attacks on cruise ships are much more likely to pose problems relating to extraterritorial jurisdiction and, consequently, questions regarding which nation's substantive civil justice laws (United States or another) will apply. On a different note, because attacks on cruise ships and ferries are more likely to focus on maximizing human casualties than on causing property damage, the nature of the claims arising from those attacks is more likely to focus on personal injuries and wrongful deaths. U.S. admiralty laws establish specific standards that will apply to resolving many of these sorts of claims, including limited liability for vessel owners under at least some circumstances. Meanwhile, terrorist attacks involving the containerized cargo system present a very different set of legal complexities. Future terrorism-related contractual disputes among commercial counterparts will optimally be limited by the general recognition of maritime threats and by explicit contract provisions (and standardized business practices) designed to apportion related risks. Tort risk, on the other hand, could be very significant in connection with an attack that uses a cargo container as a concealed-weapon platform. Such an attack could implicate a range of U.S. and foreign jurisdictions and substantive laws, in connection with a host of commercial defendants who arguably might have prevented or mitigated the attack through appropriate precautions. If such an attack were to result in mass casualties or property damage, the liability implications could conceivably be severe. The only certainties are that the civil justice system would not be able to deal with such an event quickly and that legal ambiguity would cloud the prospects of compensation for victims.

On a more abstract level, our analysis of liability issues connected with maritime terrorism suggests two more general insights. First, the specific U.S. legal rules that will apply to determining civil liability in the context of future attacks are deeply fragmented. Depending on the facts of a particular attack, applicable rules might involve any of a half-dozen statutes under U.S. admiralty law, related maritime common law precedents, or various other state or federal laws concerning negligence and wrongful death, or terrorism. This kind of legal fragmentation is problematic in itself, because it means that current and future standards for civil liability may not be consistent. That is, similarly situated plaintiffs might encounter radically different results in seeking compensation through the civil justice system, in ways fundamentally unrelated to the nature of their underlying claims or injuries. Second, a central issue at the heart of future tort claims will involve the extent to which commercial firms can be held responsible for the independent criminal acts of terrorists. This question is already being addressed in the ongoing World Trade Center litigation: Similar legal questions will likely arise in connection with a host of admiralty standards governing the conduct of passenger and commercial shipping. Expansive interpretations of the foreseeability of future attacks could lead to broad contours for liability, but with little practical guidance to firms about how to fulfill their duties of care (particularly given an abundance of low-likelihood, but highly consequential, terrorist threats).[2] Here again, the end result of liability could be to focus the risks and costs of terror-

---

[2] As we noted in Chapter Four, as negligence becomes less wedded to meaningful standards that define the duty of care for firms, then those legal standards will begin to look increasingly like strict liability rather than negligence. This is a result that is unlikely to create optimal incentives for terrorism prevention efforts by firms.

ist attacks onto maritime firms, in ways that may make insuring them fully through private markets difficult. For policymakers, this prospect raises basic questions about the appropriateness of tort liability as a mechanism for compensating terrorism injuries, and for incentivizing security measures on the part of the private sector.

It is important for us to acknowledge that our examination of civil liability issues pertaining to maritime terrorism reflects only one aspect of a broader set of institutional mechanisms and legal standards that will collectively shape the government's response to future attacks and, by implication, the financial risks and incentives faced by the private sector. Many other aspects of policy and law are likely to be important as well: security regulations and their enforcement for participants in maritime commerce, public investment in terrorism interdiction and prevention efforts, and the effectiveness of disaster response authorities also come quickly to mind. We do not address any of these other aspects of terrorism policy in this book. Nor do we explore the potential trade-offs in risk that government might achieve by emphasizing one or more of these alternative management strategies, while simultaneously reducing or eliminating civil liability. These are weighty questions for policymakers to consider. In our view, though, civil liability has a particularly central role as the established, default mechanism for compensating victims in the aftermath of an attack. Liability standards as applied to terrorism are complicated and difficult to penetrate in themselves. Yet those standards are foundational in defining the financial risks faced both by firms and by victims in connection with terrorism. To the extent that this book succeeds in outlining relevant civil liability standards, pinpointing areas of ambiguity, and analyzing some of the implications with regard to future maritime attacks, then it also provides a launching point for inquiry by policymakers into the broader domain of terrorism risk management.

Perhaps the most important implication of our work touches on the future of related commercial insurance practices. On a basic level, our analysis of maritime threats, vulnerabilities, and consequences reflects exactly the sort of calculus that insurers confront in trying to actualize related risks. Again, while our analysis cannot benchmark the absolute risk associated with specific terrorism scenarios, we nevertheless can characterize some important aspects of relative risk, across a range of potential attacks. In this sense, our work could help insurers to incorporate those risks better in the way that they structure corresponding insurance contracts (e.g., in weighting risks, defining the limits of coverage, or demanding related disclosures or covenants from policyholders). Our work might also be viewed more broadly as a blueprint for the kind of risk analysis that maritime insurers will need to undertake in the future, with regard to a wider spectrum of threats. The liability dimension of our work suggests, meanwhile, that some lines of insurance (e.g., property and casualty) will be dramatically impacted by future legal determinations regarding the extent of third-party liability for terrorism. The recent extension of TRIA highlights the continuing uncertainty that is associated with insuring against terrorist attacks, but perhaps obscures the fact that some of that uncertainty actually accrues to the U.S. civil justice system and the ambiguity of related legal standards in apportioning potentially catastrophic risks. To the extent that future reforms can simplify and clarify those legal standards, some of the pressures for government involvement in re-insurance markets might be eased.

Conclusions and Recommendations

- The greatest risks involving container shipping stem from scenarios involving radiological or nuclear detonation, or the extended disruption of operations at a port. *For radiological or nuclear detonation, effective risk management approaches must include securing nuclear materials at their points of origin.* Checking cargo containers moving through the container shipping system is impractical and imperfect because of the large number of containers and the inherent errors (both false positives and false negatives) of inspection technologies. The risks from extended disruption of ports are largely economic. *These risks are most effectively reduced through planning to facilitate the restart of ports and container shipping systems in the wake of a terrorist attack or natural disaster.*

- The greatest risks involving cruise ships and passenger ferries stem from cruise ship scenarios involving on-board bombs or food or water supply contamination and passenger ferry scenarios involving on-board bombs and USS *Cole*–style improvised explosive device attacks. Because it is essential that people be allowed to move freely on these types of vessels, it would be difficult to eliminate the risks completely. *The most effective approach for minimizing the risks, however, involves reducing the vulnerabilities of ferries and cruise ships, by auditing the soundness of VSPs and FSPs, by improving security measures at ports for passengers and luggage, and by implementing rigorous procedures for documenting crew and staff.*

- Many perceptions of maritime terrorism risks do not align with the reality of threat and vulnerabilities. First, there is little evidence that terrorists and piracy syndicates are collaborating. The economic motivations for piracy (which depend for fulfillment on the stability of maritime trade) may be in direct conflict with the motivations of terrorists (i.e., in achieving maximum disruptive effects in connection with attacks). Second, some plausible forms of maritime terrorism (e.g., sinking a cargo ship in order to block a strategic lane of communication) actually present relatively low risk, in part because the targeting of such attacks is inconsistent with the primary motivation for most terrorist groups (i.e., achieving maximum public attention through inflicted loss of life). Third, any effort to sink a freight or cruise ship would need to overcome engineering designs intended to prevent catastrophic failure of a ship's hull. Experts agree that IEDs would have limited capability to cause such failure. *These perceived threats should not motivate maritime terrorism policy.*

- Civil liability is a key aspect of the government's institutional response to maritime terrorism. Liability operates to redistribute some of the harms associated with an attack from victims to other parties who bear legal responsibility for those harms. Because terrorists are often poor prospects for recovery in civil suits seeking compensation for victims, third-party firms and property owners are likely to be targeted in postattack tort litigation. *As a result, firms engaged in maritime commerce need to recognize that they operate at risk and should investigate the extent of their own tort liability.*

- Civil liability standards in maritime terrorist attacks against the United States will likely draw on specialized rules in admiralty, particularly with regard to attacks on ferries and cruise ships. Related rules include liability standards for personal injury and death, regulatory requirements pertaining to vessel security, and statutory limits on liability for vessel owners. *Admiralty jurisdiction over these sorts of claims may preempt competing legal rules that would otherwise apply on land and may limit the compensation that victims can seek in some circumstances. Policymakers should review these rules to confirm their appropriateness in application to future terrorist attacks.*

- Maritime attacks that leverage cargo containers could target port facilities or inland locations, and subsequent supply chain disruptions could implicate a host of contractual and tort disputes. *To the extent not already standard practice, parties to commercial contracts should specifically consider and address terrorism risks in connection with those contracts.*

- A key issue in tort liability for future maritime attacks will involve the extent to which third-party defendants (i.e., firms and property owners) can be held liable for the independent actions of terrorists. The same fundamental issue could arise in connection with a host of statutory and common law rules. The traditional criterion of foreseeability in negligence provides little guidance, in the wake of the September 11 attacks, regarding the scope of related responsibilities for potential defendants. *Policymakers should carefully review the scope and rationale of third-party liability for terrorist attacks, both in regard to providing reasonable compensation to victims and in setting appropriate incentives for prevention and mitigation efforts by private firms. More broadly, policymakers should consider the pros and cons of liability as a method for dealing with terrorism risks and injuries.*

Qualitatively Assessing the Relative Risks of Maritime Terrorism

Terrorism risk does not exist without the existence of *threat*, the presence of *vulnerability*, and the potential for *consequences*. Terrorism threats exist if a group or individual has both the capability and intent to attack a target. As discussed in Chapter Three, terrorist attacks can result in human, economic, and intangible consequences. However, risks only exist if an attack can cause a change to the state of a target that results in negative consequences—in other words, if the targets are vulnerable to attack (Willis et al., 2005; Haimes, 2006).

Assessments of threat, vulnerability, and consequences can be integrated to compare terrorism risks to each other and to risks from other hazards. Ideally, one would want the risk assessment process to be fully quantitative. In such an ideal case, risks could then be broadly compared, and the effectiveness of risk management strategies could be compared to their costs. For terrorism risk, however, a fully quantitative approach would require the difficult assessment of threat in terms of the probability that terrorist attacks will occur.[1]

In the absence of information needed to support this kind of quantitative assessment, qualitative methods of risk analysis can be used. Qualitative analysis cannot guide decisions on the absolute amount of effort that should be devoted to managing risk. It can, however, guide

---

[1] Though it is difficult to assess terrorism threats, it is debatably not impossible. Bayesian decision theory has been applied to translate expert judgments of terrorists' intentions and capabilities and target vulnerabilities into probabilities of attack. For example, modeling firms like Risk Management Solutions, AIR Worldwide, and EQUECAT have developed probabilistic models to estimate terrorism risk.

priorities for risk management within the context of a specified level of effort. In other words, qualitative risk analysis cannot be used to determine how much money to spend on managing risk, but it can help answer the question of where to spend it.

In Chapters Five, Six, and Seven of this book, we present the results of a qualitative risk analysis of maritime terrorism risk scenarios involving cruise ships, passenger ferries, and container shipping. The approach, which is described in this section, relies on five basic concepts:

- Use defined, ordinal scales to assess terrorists' intent and capability, target vulnerability, and attack consequences.
- Consider the relationship between levels in the ordinal scales to have logarithmic properties such that differences between levels increase exponentially with higher scores on all scales.[2]
- Explicitly map assessments of intent and capability into assessment of threat.
- Explicitly map threat and vulnerability into assessment of attack likelihood.
- Consider both human and economic consequences.

Assessing Terrorist Intent

Chapter Two provides an overview of factors that influence the intentions of terrorist groups. That discussion forms the basis for this derivation of an anchored, ordinal scale for assessing threat.

In defining an anchored scale for intent, it is necessary to identify explicitly the terrorist organization for which the scale is attempting to match intentions. No single scale is appropriate for all groups as each

---

[2] Integrating the concept on logarithmic relationships into the definitions of anchored scales supports the intuitive notion that concern or perceptions increase exponentially as intent, vulnerabilities, capabilities, and consequence increase on these anchored scales. This notion is consistent with the observation from psychophysics that a sensation is proportional to the logarithm of its stimulus, referred to as the Weber-Fechner law (Fechner and Wundt, 1889).

has unique goals and motivations. For the purposes of this study, we use a scale of intent to capture factors that motivate terrorists affiliated with the international jihadist extremist network, which is generally viewed as constituting the greatest present threat to U.S. interests domestically and abroad. The methodology could be revised to assess threat from other terrorist groups.

The magnitude of expected consequences of attack is the most important factor motivating jihadist terrorists, with a primary goal of causing human deaths and injuries and a secondary goal of causing economic disruption.

After expected consequences, the ability to capture media attention is presumed to determine jihadists' intent in the sense that these terrorists are more prone to conduct attacks that are likely to generate significant media attention and emotive response than those that would not. Finally, assaults that also involve a venue of symbolic importance to those attacked and resonate with the global jihadist enterprise are presumed to be more attractive as targets of terrorism than those that do not.

Table A.1 describes the determinants that were used in making qualitative assessments of how maritime attack scenarios aligned with terrorists' intentions. In general, events that involved more of these factors were associated with greater intent and, as discussed above, intention is considered to increase exponentially along this scale.

On this metric, events that had consequences that were counter to terrorists' goals and objectives would receive the lowest scores (for example, strikes that are liable to result in a negative backlash on terrorist groups and hamper their ability to recruit new members or if they spark debilitating retaliatory action on the part of the attacked party). Scenarios that are more aligned with terrorists' intentions are presumed to be more likely.

Table A.1
Determinants Used in Making Qualitative Assessments of Alignment of Maritime Attack Scenarios with Terrorists' Intentions

Score	Determinants of Intent Score
1 (Low)	Outcomes would conflict with stated goals and objectives of terrorist group
2	Kills people, but without media attention, symbolic damage, or economic consequences
3	Kills people and causes economic damage, but without symbolic damage or media attention
4	Kills people and causes economic damage with media attention, but without symbolic damage
5 (High)	Kills significant numbers of people, causes significant symbolic damage, attracts significant media attention, and causes economic damage

Assessing Required Capability of Attack Scenarios

A limiting factor on terrorists' capability to attack is the training and skill of the operatives in an attack scenario. Some attack scenarios, such as suicide bombings, require relatively basic skills. In contrast, chemical, biological, nuclear, and radiological attacks all require some special skills in producing weapons, obtaining weapons, or carrying out an attack.

For the qualitative assessments of required capabilities for attack, we adopted definitions developed by Risk Management Solutions. Listed in Table A.2, these definitions were developed to assess the required skill of terrorists who were to attempt different attack scenarios. They range from low levels that require only manual labor to levels requiring highly specialized and rare skills. Scenarios that require greater skill are presumed to be less likely. As with the scale used for intent, the required capability is presumed to increase exponentially with increases in each level of this scale.

Table A.2
Determinants Used in Making Qualitative Assessments of Required Capabilities of Attack Scenarios

Score	Determinants of Required Capability Score
1 (High)	Highly specialized skills: requires highly specialized and rare skills such as operation of nuclear power plant, large-scale manufacturing, or precision or highly technical production operation in secret
2	Specialty skills: requires specialist skills such as hacking computers, piloting vehicles, or ability to plan and implement advanced coordinated operations
3	Expert military skills: requires accurately positioned explosives, accurate firing, or using more sophisticated military weapons
4	Basic military skills: requires military training skills up to basic combat level, including ability to handle personal weapons and carry out close-quarter combat
5 (Low)	Volunteer or practical skills: can be carried out using only manual labor or school-educated personnel

Assessing Vulnerability of Maritime Targets to Attack Scenarios

Vulnerability of maritime targets to attack scenarios is determined by how a ship or facility is both designed and operated. Engineering controls, such as hull designs and fencing, may be used to reduce vulnerability. Surveillance, access controls and identification cards, and inspection technologies also may reduce vulnerability.

In the qualitative assessment method used in this report, scenarios that required terrorists to counter personnel certification, surveillance, inspection, or engineered systems were assessed as being less vulnerable. The determinants used to score scenarios are listed in Table A.3. As with the previously defined scales, the vulnerability associated with a scenario is presumed to increase exponentially with increases in each level of this scale.

Table A.3
Determinants Used in Making Qualitative Assessments of Vulnerability of Targets to Attack Scenarios

Score	Determinants of Vulnerability Score
1 (Low)	Limited access to certified personnel to positions where attack can be carried out; engineering controls to prevent consequences; invasive screening, surveillance, or inspections to detect attacks
2	Limited access to certified personnel to positions where attack can be carried out; engineering controls to limit consequences; invasive screening, surveillance, or inspections to detect attacks
3	Controlled access to positions where attack can be carried out; no engineering controls to limit consequences; semi-invasive screening, surveillance, or inspections to detect attacks (e.g., check IDs, bag scanning, metal detectors)
4	Controlled access to positions where attack can be carried out; no engineering controls to limit consequences; no invasive screening, surveillance, or inspections to detect attacks (e.g., check IDs and cursory metal detectors)
5 (High)	Free access to positions where attack can be carried out; no engineering controls to limit consequences; no screening, surveillance, or inspections to detect attacks

Assessing Scenario Threat Based on Intent and Capability Scores

Qualitative assessments of threat were made based on score scenarios received based on judgments of intent and capability. The translation of these component scores into a judgment of threat was made using a normalized, multiplicative relationship shown in this equation:

$$\text{Threat} = \text{ROUND}\big(\big[\text{Intent} \times \text{Capability}\big]/5\big).$$

Threat scores are rounded using the guide in Table A.4.

Table A.4
Threat Score Rounding Guide

Normalized Threat	Rounded Score
0–1.0	1
>1–2.0	2
>2–3.0	3
>3–4.0	4
>4–5.0	5

This translation was adopted based on two intuitive observations that support a multiplicative relationship between intent and capability. First, threat only exists if both intent and capability are present. If either is absent, then no threat exists. Second, presence of high intent and high capability (i.e., a score of 5 on each scale) is intuitively *much worse* not just *worse* than a high intent (i.e., score of 5) and moderate capability (i.e., score of 3). A multiplicative relationship captures these observations more appropriately than does an additive or averaging relationship.

The resulting translation is shown in Table A.5.

Table A.5
Matrix Used to Translate Qualitative Assessments of Intent and Capability into an Assessment of Threat

Intent Score	Capability Score				
	1	2	3	4	5
1	1	1	1	1	1
2	1	1	2	2	2
3	1	2	2	3	3
4	1	2	3	4	4
5	1	2	3	4	5

Assessing Scenario Likelihood Based on Threat and Vulnerability Scores

Qualitative assessments of likelihood were made based on score scenarios received based on judgments of threat and vulnerability. The translation of these component scores into a judgment of likelihood is shown in Table A.6. This translation was derived using the same normalized, multiplicative relationship used to assess threat. The normalized multiplicative relationship was adopted for the same reasons.

Assessing Consequences of Maritime Attack Scenarios

Chapters Five, Six, Seven present risk assessments based upon both human and economic consequences of terrorist attack scenarios. Tables A.7 and A.8 present the scales used to group consequences of maritime attack scenarios.

Low ends of these scales were selected to correspond with the size of attacks that have the smallest potential consequences. For human consequences, events expected to kill or injure fewer than 10 people were given a score of 1. For economic consequences, events resulting in up to tens of millions of dollars in economic damages were given a score of 1.

Table A.6
Matrix Used to Translate Qualitative Assessments of Threat and Vulnerability into an Assessment of Likelihood

	Vulnerability				
Threat	1	2	3	4	5
1	1	1	1	1	1
2	1	1	2	2	2
3	1	2	2	3	3
4	1	2	3	4	4
5	1	2	3	4	5

The high end of the scales was established as a point above which changes in scale would not greatly influence reaction and response to the event. In terms of deaths and injuries, events expected to kill or injure more than 10,000 were given a score of 5. Events that were expected to result in hundreds of billions of dollars of economic damage were also given a score of 5.

Between these points, the ordinal scales were based on logarithmic scales of consequences. The logarithmic scales were used for two reasons. First, the tremendous uncertainty surrounding and the event-specific determinants of actual consequences of any given terrorist attack preclude assessments at a resolution much finer than an order-of-magnitude assessment. Second, logarithmic scales are widely used in descriptive scales of disasters that span a wide range of magnitude. Other common examples include the Richter scale used for earthquakes and the Saffir-Simpson Hurricane Scale.

Table A.7
Determinants Used in Making Qualitative Assessments of Human Consequences of Maritime Attack Scenarios

Score	Determinants of Human Consequences Score
1 (Low)	Fewer than 10 killed or injured
2	10–100 killed or injured
3	100–1,000 killed or injured
4	1,000–10,000 killed or injured
5 (High)	>10,000 killed or injured

Table A.8
Determinants Used in Making Qualitative Assessments of Economic Consequences of Maritime Attack Scenarios

Score	Determinants of Economic Consequences Score
1 (Low)	Up to tens of millions of dollars in economic damages
2	Hundreds of millions of dollars in economic damages
3	Billions of dollars in economic damages
4	Tens of billions of dollars in economic damages
5 (High)	Hundreds of billions of economic damages or more

Bibliography

Abt, Clark C., *The Economic Impact of Nuclear Terrorist Attacks on Freight Transport Systems in an Age of Seaport Vulnerability*, Cambridge, Mass.: Abt Associates, Inc., April 30, 2003. As of September 22, 2006:
http://www.abtassociates.com/reports/es-economic_impact_of_nuclear_terrorist_attacks.pdf

"Al-Qaeda Has Multi-Faceted Marine Strategy: Report," *Agence France Presse*, January 19, 2003.

"Al-Qaida Training Manual Shows Seaports Top Target," *WorldNetDaily*, October 30, 2003. As of October 20, 2005:
http://www.worldnetdaily.com/news/article.asp?ARTICLE_ID=35327

American Public Transportation Association, *Public Transportation Fact Book,* 57th edition, Washington, D.C.: American Public Transportation Association, April 2006. As of September 28, 2006:
http://www.apta.com/research/stats/factbook/documents/2006factbook.pdf

Anonymous Anti-Terrorism Task Force officials, interviews with the authors, Manila, November 2005.

Anonymous Anti-Terrorism Task Force officials, Manila, and former defense intelligence official, London, interviews with the authors, 2005.

Anonymous Control Risks Group (Netherlands office) personnel, interviews with the authors, Amsterdam, 2005.

Anonymous Control Risks Group (Netherlands office) personnel, interviews with the authors, London and Amsterdam, September 2005.

Anonymous Control Risks Group (Netherlands office) personnel, Amsterdam, and Department of Homeland Security Liaison attache, U.S. Embassy, Singapore, interviews with the authors, 2005.

Anonymous Control Risks Group (Netherlands office) personnel, Amsterdam, and independent maritime expert, Rotterdam, interviews with the authors, 2005.

Anonymous Control Risks Group (UK office) personnel, interviews with the authors, London, September 2005.

Anonymous Control Risks Group (UK office) personnel, London, and Department of Homeland Security Liaison attache, U.S. Embassy, London, interviews with the authors, London, 2005.

Anonymous Control Risks Group (UK office) personnel, London, and Maritime Intelligence Group analyst, Washington, D.C., interviews with the authors, 2005.

Anonymous defense antiterrorism and intelligence officials, interviews with the authors, Manila, March 2005.

Anonymous defense antiterrorism and intelligence officials and Anti-Terrorism Task Force officials, interviews with the authors, Manila, 2005.

Anonymous Department of Homeland Security Liaison attache, U.S. Embassy, interviews with the authors, London, September 2005.

Anonymous Department of Homeland Security Liaison attache, U.S. Embassy, interviews with the authors, Singapore, 2005.

Anonymous Department of Homeland Security Liaison attaches, U.S. Embassies, interviews with the authors, Singapore and London, 2005.

Anonymous Department of Homeland Security Liaison attache, U.S. Embassy, Singapore, and former defense intelligence official, London, interviews with the authors, 2005.

Anonymous former British defense intelligence official, interview with the authors, London, September 2005.

Anonymous former British defense official, interview with the authors, London, 2005.

Anonymous former British defense official and Department of Homeland Security Liaison attache, British Embassy, interviews with the authors, London, 2005.

Anonymous former defense intelligence official, interview with the authors, London, 2005.

Anonymous former defense intelligence official and Control Risks Group (UK) personnel, interviews with the authors, London, 2005.

Anonymous independent maritime expert, interview with the authors, Rotterdam, September 2005.

Anonymous Institute of Defense and Strategic Studies (IDSS) representative, interview with the authors, Singapore, September 2005.

Anonymous Institute of Defense and Strategic Studies personnel and analysts with Raytheon International (ASEAN) and Glenn Defense Marine (Asia), interviews with the authors, Singapore, September 2005.

Anonymous International Maritime Bureau personnel, interview with the authors, London, September 2005.

Anonymous International Maritime Bureau personnel and former defense intelligence official, interviews with the authors, London, 2005.

Anonymous International Maritime Bureau personnel, London, and Maritime Intelligence Group analyst, Washington, D.C., 2005.

Anonymous Lloyd's of London analysts, interviews with the authors, London, September 2005.

Anonymous Maritime Intelligence Group analyst, interviews with the authors, Washington, D.C., August 2005.

Anonymous Ministry of Foreign Affairs officials, interviews with the authors, Singapore, September 2005.

Anonymous Ministry of Foreign Affairs and Ministry of Home Affairs officials, Singapore, and Control Risks Group analysts (UK and Netherlands offices), London and Amsterdam, interviews with the authors, 2005.

Anonymous Ministry of Foreign Affairs officials and Raytheon (ASEAN) and Glenn Defense Marine (Asia) analysts, interviews with the authors, Singapore, 2005.

Anonymous Ministry of Home Affairs officials, interviews with the authors, Singapore, September 2005.

Anonymous Raytheon (ASEAN) and Glenn Defense Marine (Asia) analysts, and Control Risks Group (UK) personnel, London, 2005.

Anonymous security and terrorism analyst, Monterey Post Graduate Naval School, Monterey, Calif., 2005.

Anonymous Sri Lankan intelligence officials, interviews with the authors, Colombo, Sri Lanka, May 2004.

Anonymous Sri Lankan intelligence officials and Western diplomat, interviews with the authors, Colombo, Sri Lanka, 2005.

Anonymous UK customs and excise officials, interview with the authors, London, September 2005.

Anonymous UK customs and excise officials, former defense intelligence official, and Control Risks Group (UK) personnel, interviews with the authors, London, 2005.

Anonymous UK customs and excise officials, London; Raytheon (ASEAN) and Glenn Defense Marine (Asia) analysts, Singapore; and Control Risks Group (Netherlands) officials, Amsterdam, interviews with the authors, 2005.

Anonymous Western diplomat, interview with the authors, Colombo, Sri Lanka, May 2004.

Ant, C. Onur, "Turkish Court Charges Suspected al-Qaida Militant in Plot to Attack Israelis," The Associated Press, August 11, 2005.

"Arming the IRA: The Libyan Connection," *Economist*, March 31, 1990, p. 19.

Arnold, Bruce Gregory, *The Economic Costs of Disruptions in Container Shipments*, Washington, D.C.: Congress of the United States, Congressional Budget Office, 2006. As of September 22, 2006:
http://www.cbo.gov/ftpdocs/71xx/doc7106/03-29-Container%5FShipments.pdf

"ASEAN, EU Experts Discuss Fighting 'Terrorism at Sea,'" *Agence France Presse*, February 25, 2002.

Baker, Mark B., "'A Hard Rain's A-Gonna Fall': Terrorism and Excused Contractual Performance in a Post September 11th World," *Transnational Lawyer*, Vol. 17, 2004, pp. 1–35.

Bilmes, Linda, and Joseph Stiglitz, "War's Stunning Price Tag," *Los Angeles Times*, January 17, 2006, p. B13.

Bishop, Owen, "A 'Secure' Package? Maritime Cargo Container Security After 9/11," *Transportation Law Journal*, Vol. 29, Summer 2002, pp. 313–332.

Blanco, Kathleen Babineaux, *Hurricane Katrina: Community Rebuilding Needs and Effectiveness of Past Proposals*, testimony before the U.S. Senate Finance Committee, September 28, 2005. As of September 27, 2006:
http://www.senate.gov/~finance/hearings/testimony/2005test/092805kbtest.pdf

Brew, Nigel, "Ripples from 9/11: The U.S. Container Security Initiative and Its Implications for Australia," *Current Issues Brief*, No. 28, May 13, 2003, p. 3.

Business Research and Economic Advisors, *The Contribution of the North American Cruise Industry to the U.S. Economy in 2004*, Arlington, Va.: International Council of Cruise Lines, August 2005. As of September 21, 2006:
http://www.iccl.org/resources/2004_economic_study.pdf

Burton, Mark L., and Michael J. Hicks, *Hurricane Katrina: Preliminary Estimates of Commercial and Public Sector Damages*, Huntington, W. Va.: Center for Business and Economic Research, Marshall University, September 2005. As of September 27, 2006:
http://www.marshall.edu/cber/research/katrina/Katrina-Estimates.pdf

Campbell, Tanner, and Rohan Gunaratna, "Maritime Terrorism, Piracy and Crime," in Rohan Gunaratna, ed., *Terrorism in the Asia-Pacific: Threat and Response*, Singapore: Eastern Universities Press, 2003, pp. 70–88.

Cantor Fitzgerald, "Our Heritage," undated Web page. As of September 21, 2006:
http://www.cantor.com/heritage/

Carroll, Stephen J., Deborah R. Hensler, Jennifer Gross, Elizabeth M. Sloss, Matthias Schonlau, Allan Abrahamse, and J. Scott Ashwood, *Asbestos Litigation*, Santa Monica, Calif.: RAND Corporation, MG-162-ICJ, 2005. As of September

21, 2006:
http://www.rand.org/pubs/monographs/MG162/

Carey, Christopher E., "Maritime Transportation Security Act of 2002: Potential Civil Liabilities and Defenses," *Tulane Maritime Law Journal*, Vol. 28, No. 2, Summer 2004, pp. 295–314.

Central Intelligence Agency (CIA), *The World Factbook*, undated Web page. As of September 22, 2006:
https://www.cia.gov/cia/publications/factbook/index.html

Chalk, Peter, *West European Terrorism and Counter-Terrorism: The Evolving Dynamic*, New York: St. Martin's Press, 1996.

Chalk, Peter, Bruce Hoffman, Anna-Britt Kasupski, Robert T. Reville, *Trends in Terrorism: Threats to the United States and the Future of the Terrorism Risk Insurance Act*, Santa Monica, Calif.: RAND Corporation, MG-393-CTRMP, 2005. As of September 21, 2006:
http://www.rand.org/pubs/monographs/MG393/index.html

Clyne, Robert G., "Terrorism and Port/Cargo Security: Developments and Implications for Marine Cargo Recoveries," *Tulane Law Review*, Vol. 77, Nos. 5 and 6, June 2003, pp. 1183–1222.

Code of Federal Regulations, Title 33, Section 104.105, August 8, 2003.

The Constitution of the United States of America, Washington, D.C.: U.S. Government Printing Office, 2002. As of September 21, 2006:
http://www.gpoaccess.gov/constitution/pdf2002/006-Constitution.pdf

Coughlin, Cletus C., Jeffrey P. Cohen, and Sarosh R. Khan, *Aviation Security and Terrorism: A Review of the Economic Issues*, St. Louis, Mo.: Research Division, Federal Reserve Bank of St. Louis, 2002. As of September 27, 2006:
http://research.stlouisfed.org/wp/2002/2002-009.pdf

"Cruise Ship Listing," *CruiseCrew.com*, undated Web page. As of May 1, 2006:
http://www.cruisecrew.com/new%20ships%20listing.htm

"Cruise Ship Repels Somali Pirates," *BBC News*, November 5, 2005. As of January 30, 2006:
http://news.bbc.co.uk/2/hi/africa/4409662.stm

Cunard, "Queen Mary 2: Ship Facts," undated Web page. As of April 12, 2006:
http://www.cunard.com/QM2/default.asp?Active=about&sub=shipfacts

Cunningham, Lawrence A., "The Appeal and Limits of Internal Controls to Fight Fraud, Terrorism, and Other Ills," *Journal of Corporation Law*, Vol. 29, No. 2, Winter 2004, pp. 267–336.

Customs and Border Protection (CBP), *Fact Sheet: Cargo Container Security—U.S. Customs and Border Protection Reality*, October 2004. As of November 6, 2005:

http://www.cbp.gov/linkhandler/cgov/newsroom/fact_sheets/2004/5percent_
myth.ctt/5percent_myth.doc

Danoff, Eric, "Marine Insurance for Loss or Damage Caused by Terrorism or
Political Violence," *University of San Francisco Maritime Law Journal*, Vol. 16, No.
1, 2003–2004, pp. 61–82.

Davis, Anthony, "Tracking Tigers in Phuket: A Secret Tamil Guerrilla Base
Embarrasses Bangkok," *Asiaweek*, June 9, 2000, p. 1.

Dellapenna, Joseph, "International Terrorism: Prevention and Remedies: Legal
Remedies for Terrorist Acts," *Syracuse Journal of International Law and Commerce*,
Vol. 22, Spring 1996, pp. 13–18.

Department of Foreign Affairs and Trade, *Global Issues Brief on Economic Costs of
Terrorism*, Canberra: DFAT Economic Analytical Unit, April 7, 2003.

Diaz, Leticia, and Barry Hart Dubner, "On the Problem of Utilizing Unilateral
Action to Prevent Acts of Sea Piracy and Terrorism: A Proactive Approach to
the Evolution of International Law," *Syracuse Journal of International Law and
Commerce*, Vol. 32, No. 1, Fall 2004, pp. 1–50.

Ebersold, William B., "Industry Overview: Cruise Industry in Figures," *Touch
Briefings*, 2004.

Eedle, Paul, "G2: Inside Story: Terrorism.com: How Does al-Qaida Stay
Organised When Its Members Are in Hiding and Scattered Across the World?
Easy—It Runs a Website, Says Paul Eedle," *The Guardian* (London), July 17,
2002, G2, p. 4.

"Egypt Government, Ferry Firm Offer Compensation: Al-Salam Maritime
Transport Co Is Offering 26,000 Dollars to Family of Each Lost Person in
Tragedy," *Middle East Online*, February 8, 2006. As of May 3, 2006:
http://www.middle-east-online.com/english/?id=15699

Elegant, Simon, "The Return of Abu Sayyaf," *Time Magazine*, August 23, 2004.
As of September 27, 2006:
http://www.time.com/time/asia/magazine/article/0,13673,501040830-686107,00.
html

Enders, Walter, Todd Sandler, and Gerald F. Parise, *An Econometric Analysis of the
Impact of Terrorism on Tourism*, Glasgow: University of Glasgow, Department of
Political Economy, 1991.

English, Ben, Ian Gallagher, and Jeff Sommerfeld, "Al-Qaeda Plots Sea Assaults,"
The Courier Mail (Queensland, Australia), December 29, 2003, p. 1.

"FAQ on ISPS Code and Maritime Security," International Maritime
Organization, undated Web page. As of November 7, 2005:
http://www.imo.org/home.asp

Fechner, Gustav Theodor, and Wilhelm Max Wundt, *Elemente der Psychophysik*, 2nd ed., Leipzig: Breitkopf and Härtel, 1889.

Flynn, Stephen E., *America the Vulnerable: How Our Government Is Failing to Protect Us from Terrorism*, New York: HarperCollins, 2004a.

————, "The Neglected Home Front," *Foreign Affairs*, Vol. 83, No. 5, September/October 2004b, p. 25.

Force, Robert, *Admiralty and Maritime Law*, Washington, D.C.: Federal Judicial Center, 2004. As of September 21, 2006:
http://purl.access.gpo.gov/GPO/LPS55495

Foschi, Alga D., "The Coast Port Industry in the USA: A Key Factor in the Process of Economic Growth," Dipartimento di Scienze Economiche–Universita di Pisa, No. 46, December 2004.

Frey, Bruno S., Simon Luechinger, and Alois Stutzer, *Calculating Tragedy: Assessing the Costs of Terrorism*, Munich: CESifo, Center for Economic Studies and Ifo Institute for Economic Research, 2004.

Frittelli, John F., *Port and Maritime Security: Background and Issues for Congress*, Washington, D.C.: Congressional Research Service, RL31733, December 30, 2004. As of September 20, 2006:
http://www.ndu.edu/library/docs/crs%209.29.04.6.pdf

Garmon, Tina, "International Law of the Sea: Reconciling the Law of Piracy and Terrorism in the Wake of September 11th," *Tulane Maritime Law Journal*, Vol. 27, No. 1, Winter 2002, pp. 257–276.

Garner, Bryan A., and Henry Campbell Black, *Black's Law Dictionary*, abridged, 7th ed., St. Paul, Minn.: West Pub. Group, 2000.

Garrison, Linda, "Royal Caribbean International Names New Ultra-Voyager Cruise Ship," *About.com*, November 9, 2004. As of November 8, 2005:
http://cruises.about.com/od/cruisenews/a/041109rci_p.htm

Gash, Jim, "At the Intersection of Proximate Cause and Terrorism: A Contextual Analysis of the (Proposed) *Restatement Third of Torts'* Approach to Intervening and Superseding Causes," *Kentucky Law Journal*, Vol. 91, No. 3, 2002–2003, pp. 523–614.

Gordon, Peter, James E. Moore, III, Harry W. Richardson, and Qisheng Pan, "The Economic Impact of a Terrorist Attack on the Twin Ports of Los Angeles Long Beach," in Harry Ward Richardson and Peter Gordon, eds., *The Economic Impacts of Terrorist Attacks*, Cheltenham, UK, and Northampton, Mass.: Edward Elgar, 2005, pp. 262–286.

Grier, Peter, and Faye Bowers, "How Al Qaeda Might Strike the US by Sea," *The Christian Science Monitor*, May 15, 2003, p. 2.

Gruendel, Robert J., and Angelique M. Crain, "The Maritime Contract and Admiralty Jurisdiction: Recent Developments Help Clarify an Inherently Confused Landscape," *Tulane Law Review*, Vol. 77, Nos. 5 and 6, June 2003, pp. 1235–1264.

Haimes, Yacov Y., "On the Definition of Vulnerabilities in Measuring Risks to Infrastructures," *Risk Analysis*, Vol. 26, No. 2, April 2006, pp. 293–296.

Halberstam, Malvina, "Terrorism on the High Seas: The Achille Lauro, Piracy and the IMO Convention on Maritime Safety," *American Journal of International Law*, Vol. 82, No. 2, April 1988, pp. 269–310.

Hall, Peter V., "'We'd Have to Sink the Ships': Impact Studies and the 2002 West Coast Port Lockout," *Economic Development Quarterly*, Vol. 18, No. 4, November 2004, pp. 354–367.

Herbert-Burns, Rupert, "Terrorism in the Early 21st Century Maritime Domain," in Joshua Ho and Catherine Zara Raymond, eds., *The Best of Times, The Worst of Times: Maritime Security in the Asia-Pacific*, Singapore: World Scientific, 2005, pp. 155–178.

Herbert-Burns, Rupert, and Lauren Zucker, "Drawing the Line Between Piracy and Maritime Terrorism," *Janes Intelligence Review*, September 2004, p. 3.

Hochberg, Adam, "Louisiana Lawmakers Ponder Budget Woes," *Weekend Edition Sunday*, National Public Radio, November 13, 2005. As of September 21, 2006: http://www.npr.org/templates/story/story.php?storyId=5010945

Hoge, James F., and Gideon Rose, *How Did This Happen: Terrorism and the New War*, New York: PublicAffairs, 2001.

"Hostage Taking Action by Pro-Chechen Rebels Impairs Turkey's Image," *People's Daily*, China, April 24, 2001.

ICG—*see* International Crisis Group.

"IDF Seizes PA Weapons Ship," *Jewish Virtual Library*, January 4, 2002. As of December 7, 2005: http://www.jewishvirtuallibrary.org/jsource/Peace/paship.html

Ijaz, Mansoor, "The Maritime Threat from al-Qaeda," *Financial Times* (London), October 20, 2003, p. 21.

In re September 11 Litigation, 280 F. Supp. 2d 279, September 9, 2003.

"Insurance Claims to Exceed $110m," *Lloyd's List*, September 29, 2004.

International Council of Cruise Lines, "A Partner in U.S. Growth," undated Web page. As of November 7, 2005: http://www.iccl.org/resources/economicstudies.cfm

International Crisis Group, *Al-Qaeda in Southeast Asia: The Case of the "Ngruki Network" in Indonesia*, Jakarta and Brussels: International Crisis Group, August 8, 2002.

———, *Jemaah Islamiyah in South East Asia: Damaged but Still Dangerous*, Jakarta and Brussels: International Crisis Group, August 26, 2003.

International Group of P&I Clubs, IMO Jakarta Meeting on the Straits of Malaca and Singapore: Enhancing Safety, Security and Environmental Protection, September 7 and 8, 2005.

International Maritime Organization, *Reports on Acts of Piracy and Armed Robbery Against Ships*, September 4, 2003. As of September 21, 2006: http://www.imo.org/includes/blastDataOnly.asp/data_id%3D8084/40.pdf

"ISPS Code Status Update 01," International Maritime Organization, undated Web page. As of November 7, 2005: http://www.imo.org/home.asp

Ito, Harumi, and Darin Lee, "Assessing the Impact of the September 11 Terrorist Attacks on U.S. Airline Demand," *Journal of Economics and Business*, Vol. 57, No. 1, January–February 2005, pp. 75–95.

Jackson, Brian A., and Lloyd Dixon, unpublished research, Santa Monica, Calif.: RAND Corporation, December 2005.

Jehl, Douglas, and David Johnston, "In Video Message, bin Laden Issues Warning to U.S.," *The New York Times*, October 30, 2004, p. 1.

Jenkins, Brian, Bonnie Cordes, Karen Gardela, and Geraldine Petty, "A Chronology of Terrorist Attacks and Other Criminal Actions Against Maritime Targets," in B. A. H. Parritt, ed., *Violence at Sea: A Review of Terrorism, Acts of War, and Piracy, and Countermeasures to Prevent Terrorism*, Paris: International Chamber of Commerce Pub., 1986, pp. 63–86.

Jesus, H. E. José Luis, "Protection of Foreign Ships Against Piracy and Terrorism at Sea: Legal Aspects," *The International Journal of Marine and Coastal Law*, Vol. 18, No. 3, 2003, pp. 363–400.

Keeton, Page, and William Lloyd Prosser, *Prosser and Keeton on the Law of Torts*, 5th ed., St. Paul, Minn.: West Pub. Co., 1984.

Knight, Rory F., and Deborah J. Pretty, *The Impact of Catastrophes on Shareholder Value*, Oxford: Templeton College, 1997.

Köknar, Ali M., "Maritime Terrorism: A New Challenge for NATO," *Energy Security*, January 24, 2005. As of December 8, 2005: http://www.iags.org/n0124051.htm

Lakdawalla, Darius N., and George Zanjani, *Insurance, Self-Protection, and the Economics of Terrorism*, Santa Monica, Calif.: RAND Corporation, WR-171-ICJ,

2004. As of September 22, 2006:
http://www.rand.org/pubs/working_papers/WR171/

Lawson, Catherine T., and Roberta E. Weisbrod, "Ferry Transport: The Realm of Responsibility for Ferry Disasters in Developing Nations," *Journal of Public Transportation*, Vol. 8, No. 4, 2005, pp. 17–31. As of September 22, 2006: http://www.nctr.usf.edu/jpt/pdf/JPT%208-4S%20Lawson.pdf

Lewinsohn, Jonathan, "Note: Bailing Out Congress: An Assessment and Defense of the Air Transportation Safety and System Stabilization Act of 2001," *The Yale Law Journal*, Vol. 115, November 2005, pp. 438–490.

(State of) Louisiana, ex rel. William J. Guste, Jr., Attorney General, et al., Plaintiffs, Ventura Trading Company, Ltd., Inc., et al., Plaintiffs-Appellants, v. M/V Testbank, Her Engines, Tackle, Apparel, Her Owners, etc., et al., Partenreederei M/S Charlotta, etc., et al., Defendants-Appellees, 752 F. 2d 1019, February 11, 1985.

Maersk Line, "Virtual Vessel Tour," undated Web page. As of May 4, 2006: http://www.maerskline.com/link/?page=brochure&path=/about_us/vessel_tour

Manalo, Eusaquito P., *The Philippine Response to Terrorism: The Abu Sayyaf Group*, Monterey, Calif.: Naval Postgraduate School, 2004.

McGeown, Kate, "Aceh Rebels Blamed for Piracy," *BBC News Online*, September 8, 2003. As of May 1, 2006: http://news.bbc.co.uk/1/hi/world/asia-pacific/3090136.stm

Mellor, Justin S. C., "Missing the Boat: The Legal and Practical Problems of the Prevention of Maritime Terrorism," *American University International Law Review*, Vol. 18, No. 2, 2002, pp. 341–398.

Mintz, John, "15 Freighters Believed to Be Linked to Al Qaeda: U.S. Fears Terrorists at Sea; Tracking Ships Is Difficult," *The Washington Post*, December 31, 2002, p. A1.

Moragne v. State Marine Lines, Inc., et al., 398 U.S. 375, June 15, 1970.

Newman, Rick, "Full Steam Ahead: In the New Age of What Ifs, Here Is What Cruise Liners Are Doing to Keep You Safe," *National Geographic Traveler*, January/February 2003, p. 12.

Norfolk Shipbuilding and Drydock Corporation v. Celestine Garris, Administratrix of the Estate of Christopher Garris, Deceased, 532 U.S. 811, June 4, 2001.

Organization for Economic Cooperation and Development (OECD), *Security in Maritime Transport: Risk Factors and Economic Impact*, Paris: OECD, July 2003. As of September 22, 2006: http://www.oecd.org/dataoecd/19/61/18521672.pdf

Linda C. Palka, Appellant, v. Servicemaster Management Services Corporation, Respondent, 83 N.Y. 2nd 579, May 5, 1994.

Penders, Michael J., and William L. Thomas, "Ecoterror: Rethinking Environmental Security After September 11," *National Resources and Environment (NR&E)*, Winter 2002, pp. 159–207. As of October 18, 2005: http://abanet.org/environ/pubs/nre/specissue/pendersthomas.pdf

The Pennsylvania, 86 U.S. 125, October 1873.

Percival, Bronson, *Indonesia and the United States: Shared Interests in Maritime Security*, Washington, D.C.: United States–Indonesia Society, June 2005.

Perl, Raphael, and Ronald O'Rourke, *Terrorist Attack on USS Cole: Background and Issues for Congress*, Washington, D.C.: Congressional Research Service, 01-RS-20721, January 30, 2001.

Pollak, Richard, *The Colombo Bay*, New York: Simon and Schuster, 2004.

Public Law 109-144, Terrorism Risk Insurance Extension Act of 2005, December 22, 2005. As of September 22, 2006: http://frwebgate.access.gpo.gov/cgi-bin/getdoc.cgi?dbname=109_cong_public_laws&docid=f:publ144.109.pdf

Quentin, Sophia, "Shipping Activities: Targets of Maritime Terrorism," *MIRMAL*, Vol. 2, January 20, 2003. As of October 18, 2005: http://www.derechomaritimo.info/pagina/mater.htm

Raymond, Catherine Zara, *Maritime Terrorism in Southeast Asia: A Risk Assessment*, Singapore: Institute of Defence and Strategic Studies, Nanyang Technological University, 2005.

Republic of the Philippines, Office of the Press Secretary, "2 Abu Sayyaf Bandits in Super Ferry Bombing Presented to GMA," October 11, 2004. As of April 7, 2006: http://www.news.ops.gov.ph/archives2004/oct11.htm#2%20Abu%20Sayyaf

Reynolds, Melinda L., "Landowner Liability for Terrorist Acts," *Case Western Reserve Law Review*, Vol. 47, No. 1, Fall 1996, pp. 155–206.

Richardson, Michael, *A Time Bomb for Global Trade: Maritime-Related Terrorism in an Age of Weapons of Mass Destruction*, Singapore: Institute for Southeast Asian Studies, 2004.

Robins Dry Dock and Repair Company v. Flint et al., 275 U.S. 303, December 12, 1927.

Rosoff, Heather, and Detlof von Winterfeldt, *A Risk and Economic Analysis of Dirty Bomb Attacks on the Ports of Los Angeles and Long Beach*, Los Angeles, Calif.: Center for Risk and Economic Analysis of Terrorism Events, University of Southern California, 05-027, October 23, 2005. As of August 10, 2006: http://www.usc.edu/dept/create/reports/Report05027.pdf

Rue, Thomas S., "The Uniqueness of Admiralty and Maritime Law," *Tulane Law Review*, Vol. 79, Nos. 5 and 6, June 2005, pp. 1127–1148.

Sakhuja, Vijay, "Challenging Terrorism at Sea," *Institute of Peace and Conflict Studies*, January 19, 2002. As of September 21, 2006:
http://www.ipcs.org/Terrorism_kashmirLevel2.
jsp?action=showView&kValue=131&subCatID=1014&status=article&mod=g

"Santa Maria Hijacking," *Wikipedia, The Free Encyclopedia*, undated Web page. As of August 2, 2006:
http://en.wikipedia.org/wiki/Santa_Maria_hijacking

Saunders, J., "Marine Vulnerability and the Terrorist Threat," London: International Maritime Bureau, 2003.

Schoenbaum, Thomas J., and Jessica C. Langston, "An All Hands Evolution: Port Security in the Wake of September 11th," *Tulane Law Review*, Vol. 77, Nos. 5 and 6, June 2003, pp. 1333–1370.

Schulkin, Andrew, "Safe Harbors: Crafting an International Solution to Cruise Ship Pollution," *Georgetown International Environmental Law Review*, Vol. 15, No. 1, 2002, pp. 105–132.

Senior Counter-Terrorism Course (SCTC), Asia Pacific Center for Security Studies (APCSS), Honolulu, HI, September 1, 2005.

Sheffi, Yosef, *The Resilient Enterprise: Overcoming Vulnerability for Competitive Advantage*, Cambridge, Mass.: MIT Press, 2005.

Shenon, Philip, "After the War: Security: U.S. Widens Checks at Foreign Ports," *The New York Times*, June 12, 2003, p. A1.

Sheppard, Ben, "Maritime Security Measures," *Janes Intelligence Review*, March 2003.

Sinai, Joshua, "Future Trends in Worldwide Maritime Terrorism," *Connections: The Quarterly Journal*, Vol. 3, No. 1, March 2004, pp. 49–66. As of September 20, 2006:
http://www.ciaonet.org/olj/co/co_mar04/co_mar04e.pdf

Sitilides, John, "U.S. Strikes Expose Emerging Regional Threats," *The HR-Net Forum: The Washington Monitor*, August 28, 1998. As of May 1, 2006:
http://www.hri.org/forum/intpol/wm.98-08-28.html

Skinner, Jerome L., "An American Civil Law Response to International Terror," *Journal of Air Law and Commerce*, Vol. 69, Summer 2004, pp. 545–560.

Smith, Tamsin, "Policing Spain's Southern Coast," *BBC News*, May 18, 2004. As of December 8, 2005:
http://news.bbc.co.uk/2/hi/africa/3582217.stm

Staring, Graydon S., "Insurance and Reinsurance of Marine Interests in the New Age of Terrorism," *Tulane Law Review*, Vol. 77, Nos. 5 and 6, June 2003, pp. 1371–1406.

"Summary of Report," *The Manila Times*, April 12, 2004. As of September 27, 2006:
http://www.westerndefense.org/articles/PhilippineRepublic/may04.htm

"Terrorism in Southeast Asia—The Threat and Response," conference, Singapore, April 12–13, 2006.

Thompson, Michael, and Gordon Fry, "Containing the Containers: Assessing Marine Risk Accumulation," *Catastrophe and Risk Management*, September 2004.

Tillinghast-Towers Perrin, *U.S. Tort Costs: 2004 Update—Trends and Findings on the Cost of the U.S. Tort System*, New York: Tillinghast-Towers Perrin, 2004. As of August 16, 2006:
http://www.towersperrin.com/TILLINGHAST/publications/reports/Tort_2004/Tort.pdf

Uniform Commercial Code, Section 2-319, F.O.B. and F.A.S. Terms.

———, Section 2-615, Excuse by Failure of Presupposed Conditions.

United Nations, *United Nations Convention on the Law of the Sea*, December 10, 1982. As of September 21, 2006:
http://www.un.org/Depts/los/convention_agreements/texts/unclos/unclos_e.pdf

———, *Convention for the Suppression of Unlawful Acts Against the Safety of Maritime Navigation*, March 10, 1988. As ofo September 21, 2006:
http://www.unodc.org/unodc/terrorism_convention_maritime_navigation.html

U.S. Code, Title 28, Section 1333, Admiralty, Maritime, and Prize Cases, May 24, 1949.

U.S. Code Service, Title 46, Appendix, Section 181, Liability of Vessel Owner's Liability, February 28, 1871.

———, Title 46, Appendix, Section 190, Stipulations Relieving from Liability for Negligence, February 13, 1893.

———, Title 46, Appendix, Section 1300, Carriage of Goods by Sea Act, April 16, 1936.

———, Title 46, Appendix, Section 688, Recovery for Injury to or Death of Seaman, December 29, 1982.

———, Title 33, Section 901, Longshore and Harbor Workers' Compensation Act, September 28, 1984.

———, Title 46, Appendix, Section 761, Death on the High Seas Act, April 5, 2000a.

———, Title 49, Section 40101, Air Transportation Safety and System Stabilization Act, April 5, 2000b.

———, Title 6, Appendix, Section 101, Homeland Security Act of 2002, November 25, 2002a.

————, Title 6, Section 442, Litigation Management, November 25, 2002b.

————, Title 46, Sections 70101–70117, Port Security sections, November 25, 2002c.

————, Title 46, Section 71103, Port Security Civil Penalty, July 11, 2006.

U.S. Department of Homeland Security, *Budget-in-Brief: Fiscal Year 2006*, Washington, D.C.: Department of Homeland Security, 2006. As of May 4, 2006: http://www.dhs.gov/interweb/assetlibrary/Budget_BIB-FY2006.pdf

U.S. Department of Transportation, *U.S. Economic Growth and the Marine Transportation System: A White Paper Sponsored by the Marine Transportation System National Advisory Council*, December 18, 2000. As of September 27, 2006: http://www.mtsnac.org/docs/mtswhite.pdf

Villaviray, Johnna, "When Christians Embrace Islam," *The Manila Times*, November 17, 2003. As of September 28, 2006: http://www.manilatimes.net/others/special/2003/nov/17/20031117spel.html

"Virus Strikes Cruise Ship: Nearly 250 Sickened by Norwalk-like Virus," *CNN. com*, January 22, 2005. As of January 30, 2006: http://www.cnn.com/2005/TRAVEL/01/22/cruise.virus/

Waller, Mark J., and Jane M. Warrington, "9/11: A Destructive Lesson in Construction," *Insurance Law Journal*, Vol. 15, 2004, pp. 241–258.

Warouw, Mirelle, "The Threat Against Maritime Assets: A Review of Historical Cases, Operational Patterns and Indicators," unpublished paper prepared for the Institute of Defense and Strategic Studies, 2005.

Warshauer, Irving J., and Stevan C. Dittman, "The Uniqueness of Maritime Personal Injury and Death Law," *Tulane Law Review*, Vol. 79, Nos. 5 and 6, June 2005, pp. 1163–1226.

Watkins, Eric, "Shipping Fraud Heightens Terror Threat," *BBC News*, February 6, 2002. As of September 27, 2006: http://news.bbc.co.uk/2/hi/asia-pacific/1804146.stm

"What al-Qaida Could Do with 'Terror Navy,'" *WorldNetDaily*, October 20, 2003. As of December 8, 2005: http://www.wnd.com/news/article.asp?ARTICLE_ID=35157

Whitaker, Brian, "Bali Bombing: Tanker Blast Was Work of Terrorists," *The Guardian* (London), October 17, 2002, p. 6.

Wilkinson, Paul, "Terrorism and the Maritime Environment" in B. A. H. Parritt, ed., *Violence at Sea: A Review of Terrorism, Acts of War, and Piracy, and Countermeasures to Prevent Terrorism*, Paris: International Chamber of Commerce Pub., 1986, pp. 27–41.

Willis, Henry H., Andrew R. Morral, Terrence K. Kelly, and Jamison Jo Medby, *Estimating Terrorism Risk*, Santa Monica, Calif.: RAND Corporation, MG-388-

RC, 2005. As of September 20, 2006:
http://www.rand.org/pubs/monographs/MG388/index.html

Willis, Henry H., and David S. Ortiz, *Evaluating the Security of the Global Containerized Supply Chain*, Santa Monica, Calif.: RAND Corporation, TR-214-RC, 2004. As of September 20, 2006:
http://www.rand.org/pubs/technical_reports/TR214/

Wing, Maria J., "Rethinking the Easy Way Out: Flags of Convenience in the Post–September 11th Era," *Tulane Maritime Law Journal*, Vol. 28, No. 1, Winter 2003, pp. 173–190.

"World Briefing Middle East: Security Fears Keep Israeli Ships from Turkey," *The New York Times*, August 9, 2005, p. A9.

Wrightson, Margaret T., *Maritime Security: New Structures Have Improved Information Sharing, but Security Clearances Processing Requires Further Attention: Report to Congressional Requesters*, Washington, D.C.: U.S. Government Accountability Office, GAO-05-394, 2005.

Zycher, Benjamin, *A Preliminary Benefit/Cost Framework for Counterterrorism Public Expenditures*, Santa Monica, Calif.: RAND Corporation, MR-1693-RC, 2003. As of September 21, 2006:
http://www.rand.org/pubs/monograph_reports/MR1693/